WAKE UP CHURCH!

Companion

Study Guide And New Revelation

Patricia S. Welsh

ISBN: 978-1-971940-09-0 (sc)
ISBN: 978-1-971940-10-6 (e)

Rev. date: 02/03/2026

FROM THE AUTHOR

"I believe that reading and studying more about WAKE UP CHURCH! will help you mature in your faith and give you confidence to be who you were created to be. Here are some reviews from people who have read the book.

"A Life-Changing Read! Patricia's book is full of wisdom and insight that brings you closer to God. It makes you realize that there is so much more to our faith than we may have understood. This book will uplift and guide you to a deeper understanding of your purpose in God's plan." - Kristi Martin

"Patricia's book doesn't just teach – it encourages and motivates. By exploring hidden Biblical truths, it helps you unlock the "more" that God has in store for your life. It's not just about religion but about personal growth, purpose, and finding meaning. -Henri Schmidt

"This book provides a deeper understanding of the Bible's teachings and how they relate to your life today. Patricia's words are both gentle and profound, giving you the tools to embrace God's "more" for you. A must-read for anyone looking to enhance their faith journey!" -Ella Fischer

"This book delivers a fresh perspective on faith and purpose. Patricia's journey and the hidden Biblical truths she shares will inspire you to seek out the "more" God has for your life. It's a beautifully written and spiritually enriching read!" -Cheska Muller

"I truly appreciate the comments these people are sharing about WAKE UP CHURCH! I am blessed knowing that they have been inspired and encouraged by it." - Patricia S. Welsh

INSTRUCTIONS

If you have not read WAKE UP CHURCH! please do so before you use this Study Guide. Let the revelation presented soak into your mind and heart. On a separate paper, as you read, write down any questions you may have, and any comments that come to mind. When you begin your Study Guide, check off any questions that are answered, and make note of anything pertaining to your written comments. By reading the book first, it will help you to know where you are in your level of maturity. It is important to know this.

The purpose of the Guide is to help you grow in your faith and mature in your understanding. It will help you to understand the nuances of the topics covered in WAKE UP CHURCH!, and it will delve deeper into the topics that were presented in the book; new revelations. As you proceed, you should find yourself maturing in your faith.

As you study, do not forget to talk to the Lord. Ask Him to calm your mind and to give you wisdom and understanding, to make the topic clearer, to help you apply what you are learning to your daily life, etc. This is a journey you need to walk with God, developing a relationship with Him, and you cannot leave Him out of the process.

- When you are given pages to read, they are from WAKE UP CHURCH! Please refer to them while you study.

- When Bible verses are given, please read them before continuing. There may be questions asked about them.

- When there are questions, please take the time to thoughtfully answer them when they are asked and be as honest as you can. This is the only way to know where you stand and know what you must do to mature.

Doing these three things will provide a much better understanding of what you are studying.

Questions are based on the book pages read, unless they refer to a scripture. They are numbered in each study. It is recommended that you get a notebook to write down your answers and to complete your assignments.

As you proceed write down thoughts you may have, definitions of words you may not understand, questions you have and anything else you may want to review later.

As you do these studies, take your time. You do not have to complete them in a certain amount of time. Some may be able to completed in one sitting; others may take longer. The key is to take to heart what you are studying and then use it in your daily lives; live it out. Make it your lifestyle.

Pages to read are different between the first and second editions of WAKE UP CHURCH! First edition pages will be listed like this: (1st) 1- 4 The second edition pages will be listed like this: (2nd) 2-5.

NOTE: The answer key for this Study Guide can be found at patriciaswelshauthor.com.

If WAKE UP CHURCH! and this Study Guide make a difference in your life, I encourage you to leave reviews for both of them on Amazon. Most people read reviews before they decide to read a book. Encourage them to find their purposes.

- Patricia S. Welsh

CONTENTS

INTRODUCTION

This is a very deep, true study with many thought-provoking questions, scriptures, and assignments. It is not just filling in blanks with one-word answers. You are about to enter a journey that will take you into a deeper relationship with the Lord. These studies will serve as a personal guide during your journey.

I was a child in Christ when I started my journey, even though I was 67 years old. There was so much that I did not understand, or even know, because I was not taught the whole Truth. WAKE UP CHURCH! was written from conversations I had with God. He was teaching me basic truths I should have already known.

A baby is not born with the ability to eat solid food. Babies are born only able to digest milk. As they grow, they can eat soft foods. Solid food is added as the child matures. Our walk in faith is similar in many ways. When I started my journey with God, I was still childlike in my understanding. So, God had to feed me with soft food. WAKE UP CHURCH! is that soft food I needed to be able to help me mature in my faith.

(Hebrews 5:11-14). 1 What does the verse say the immature, those on milk, are unskilled in?

2 Solid food is for the mature, who are they?

Time for solid food. Let the journey begin. - PS Welsh

GROWING

You are teaching what I must know,
Which helps my trust to grow
In Jesus the Son,
Who has already won
The battle with our foe.
                              - Patricia S. Welsh

READ THE BOOK'S INTRODUCTION.

As you can see, I did some soul searching before I started my spiritual journey with God. I believe it would be beneficial for you also. Think about your life and ask yourself questions like these and contemplate on them: Am I satisfied with what I know about God? Do I feel like something is missing? Do I understand the verses I have read? Do they make sense based on what I have been taught? Do I feel an emptiness inside me? Do I really understand who Jesus is and what He accomplished with His sacrifice? What would I like to change about me? Do I need to learn more about my relationship with God and others? Is there something more? You may find it beneficial to start a personal journal of your own.

These studies will help you know who you are, understand where you are, and help you become the person God created you to be and do what He created you to do. As you begin your journey, remember the message God gave in the book's introduction, a message to all people: He wants to bless us beyond measure, and He wants a personal relationship with every person. He misses people so much that He sent Jesus to save us from eternal death, so that we can have eternal life with Him. HE LOVES US BEYOND MEASURE!

THINGS TO THINK ABOUT BEFORE THE STUDY

What do I want to accomplish with these studies? Am I a Christian? If so, how do I know?

If you are not sure how to answer those questions now, you should know by the end of this WAKE UP CHURCH! Study Guide.

The next section will include a teaching or conversation in which God delves deeper into what was covered in the study, the "solid food" so to speak. When you believe you are ready to go deeper into the topics covered in the study, read this section in the study. In the conversations, my words will be in normal print, God's will be in Italics.

Meat and Potatoes

(A message for you and for Satan)

It is time for some meat. My people must grow up in their faith, it is time to feed on solid food, not baby food anymore. Voice my Word, my Truth all the time. Make it a reality in the physical realm. The world needs that, even though many do not realize that.

Everyone has a built in need to know me; a yearning to know me. It is in their DNA. Satan wants to rip that yearning out of people. His minions want to destroy it completely because Satan wants it destroyed; needs it destroyed.

You know what I say to that? Hah! That yearning is only going to get stronger as the world gets darker. And I will manifest in this

realm like never before. You think you are going to rip me out of people, Satan? I AM going to show the world just how fast I can rip you out. You have gone too far. You have been playing god, but I AM GOD! And soon all the world will know it!

The world will know the truth about you; Not your supposed truth of you being a king, the ruler, a god. NO! They will look at you and see a defeated, fallen angel, with no power or authority. They will see a loser!

I have spoken, and so it is! Amen!

Study 1 - He Wants Us to Know Him

1. Did you know that God wants to be a personal friend to you?

PAGES (1st) 1- 4   (2nd) 1- 4

2. List the 5 reasons God wants that personal relationship with you.

The following verses support what God says about the reasons He wants a relationship with you. (1 Corinthians 1:9) **3.** What were you called into?

4. Who called you into this?

The important thing to remember here is that the Son of God, Jesus, is God in physical form. When we are called into a fellowship with Jesus, we are called into fellowship with God.

(John 17:3) This is the most important thing we can know about God. It is that personal spiritual relationship with Him that gives us eternal life. [More about eternal life later.] It is not just knowing about Him but knowing Him on a personal level.

(Isaiah 30:18) **5.** According to the scripture, what is the LORD? He wants us to long for that personal spiritual relationship as well. He waits for that.

(Luke 10:25-28) **6.** What did Jesus tell the lawyer after he answered Jesus' question correctly? Jesus said that the law the lawyer spoke of was the greatest command of all.

(Matthew 22:37-40) These two commandments are about love, God's unconditional love for us and through us to others.

7. What depends on those two commandments?

(Job 11:13-19) These are the benefits of giving your heart to God. The verse says you will feel secure. **8.** Why?

Jesus said that to love your neighbors as you love yourself is the second greatest command. (Luke 10:29-37) **G**. Who is your neighbor?

(John 3:16) [Note: If the translation you are reading says "only son" add the word begotten, because it is the meaning of the original text. [Some translations leave that word out.] **BEGOTTEN: born of a woman.** (Dancey, 2023) The third chapter in Luke recites the lineage of Jesus. (Luke 3:38) **10.** How does this verse refer to Adam? Adam was God's son but not born of a woman.

God missed us so much that He sacrificed His Son to save you and to redeem you so that you could have a relationship with Father God. How extraordinary that is! **10a** Write down your thoughts about that.

Now think about this. How would you feel watching your child being spit on, punched in the face, a crown of thorns being jammed upon the head, being stripped, and flogged with a scourge whip that ripped out pieces of flesh, sometimes to the bone? Would it tear out your heart watching your child struggling to carry a heavy cross member that was rubbing against shoulders torn from the beating, already dying from loss of blood and fluids? That would cause ischemia in some parts of the body from lack of nutrients and oxygen. Not only does it cause exhaustion from lack of oxygen—it would be a struggle to just put one foot in front of the other— it is very painful as well.

Would you be sobbing as your child was stripped completely naked and nails hammered into what was considered part of the hands, the beginning of the wrists? Would you feel sympathy pain as your child's shoulders and elbows became dislocated from the weight of the body as they raised the cross member? Would you cringe as nails were driven into the feet? Would you hold your breath as your child pushed up against torn feet just to expel air from the lungs so the next breath could be taken in, as bare wounds scrape along the wood of the cross?

Incidentally, for a person to speak, air must pass over the vocal cords during exhalation. The Gospels note that Jesus spoke seven times from the cross. It is amazing that despite His excruciating pain, He pushes up to say, "Forgive them." (Shrier, 2002)

Would you feel helpless as extreme thirst hit your child as the sun beat down on an unsheltered body? Would you fall to your knees as your child cried, "It is finished!" and died, not only from blood loss, but from slow suffocation as well? Those of you that have asthma attacks may have a better understanding than the rest of us. Father God had to bear the heartache of watching His son go through all that, and Jesus volunteered for it. He had a choice. He did not want to go through all that torture and pain. He agonized about it so much that He sweated blood while praying to His Father in Heaven.

(Luke 22:44) **11.** What does the verse say about his sweat? Thankfully, He chose to do His Father's will.

The sweating of blood is called **HEMATOHIDROSIS, caused by ruptured capillary blood vessels that feed the sweat glands, which cause then to exude blood; it occurs under conditions of extreme physical or emotional stress.** (J. Dermatol et. al, 2013)

I know it is difficult to read the last eleven paragraphs, but we, living in modern times, cannot grasp the terrible torture Jesus suffered. We do not know how devastating his sacrifice really was to Him. Every painting we see of Him on the cross is so far from reality. They show barely any blood dripping, but He was bleeding to death from terrible wounds all over His body, including His head, because of the crown of thorns jammed on it. Head wounds bleed profusely.

When you look at the face in the paintings, you know that it is Jesus. However, in reality, He was so bruised and swollen that you could barely recognize His face as a human face.

(Isaiah 52:14) Jesus was hardly recognizable as a human being. The paintings show Jesus wearing a loincloth. In reality, He was

stripped naked, exposed, and hung for all to see! He suffered the

shame of the cross because He took the shame of our sins upon Himself. When they took His robe off, they were tearing it away from the dried blood which opened up all those terrible wounds again. Imagine how agonizing that would have been.

Here is the most amazing thing: He knew what He was going to go through because He had seen people who had been flogged, and He had seen many crucifixions. He lived under Roman rule that used crucifixion, but it was invented by the Persians between 300-400 BC. It is quite possibly the most painful death ever invented by humankind. The English language derives the word "excruciating" from crucifixion, acknowledging it as a form of slow, painful suffering. (Shrier, 2002)

You will never really appreciate how much Jesus genuinely loves you until you fully understand the agonizing and shameful punishment that He suffered on your behalf. God deserves your heart, your love, and your total devotion because of His unconditional love for you, and for the unbelievable, tortuous sacrifice Jesus made on your behalf.

What are your thoughts about what was mentioned about the crucifixion and how you think you would react if your loved one was being crucified?

I highly recommend that you read the article about crucifixion that is referenced at end of this guide. It tells what Jesus went through from the scientific point-of-view. I believe it will increase your appreciation of how huge a sacrifice Jesus made on your behalf. Nothing else even comes close to showing you just how much and unconditionally He loves you.

According to the book, why does God want you to do His will?

What does God say you are because you are a part of His family? This requires a personal relationship with God. **15.** Do you consider yourself worthy to have a personal relationship with God? **16.** Why or why not?

17. Did you know that when you accept Jesus as Lord of your life, God becomes your Father because He adopts you into His family?

(John 1:12-13) **18.** Who are the children of God born of? Notice that it says Jesus gave you the right to become a child of God, it does not say that you *will* become a child of God. It is a choice you must make.

(John 5:24) **1G.** Why do people with eternal life not come into judgement? Notice that Jesus did not say that you must believe that Father God exists, but that you must believe Him; believe what He says in His Word. The Bible is His written Word; Jesus is His living Word.

(John 17:17) Jesus is praying to Father God on behalf of the disciples, and then He acknowledges Father God's Word. **20.** What does Jesus say about Father God's Word?

If you believe His Word, then you will do His will. This proves to Him and others that you do believe Him. Jesus gave you the right to have eternal life when you received Him and believed in His name, now you follow Him for He is the way to eternal life.

(John 14:6) **21.** According to the verse, how does someone come to the Father? You then must believe Father God's Word and do His will. You choose to have eternal life by doing God's will. This means you have made Jesus the Lord of your life, because He only did Father God's will, and now you live your life like Jesus, living out the Truth according to what the Bible says, because God's Word is Truth.

Ask yourself what Jesus would do. When you live out God's Truth, you have stopped living from the worldly point-of-view and are living from the spiritual point-of-view. You stop being led by emotions and are now led by Holy Spirit. God adopts you into His Family and you now have His authority to make a difference in the world. You become worthy when you become His child, which means you now live in eternal life, representing Him, and are now a citizen of heaven.

(Philippians 3:20) Paul says we are citizens of heaven now. We are ambassadors of heaven, here on earth, while we await the second coming of Jesus.

THINGS TO THINK ABOUT BEFORE THE NEXT STUDY

Have I really given much thought to what it must have been like for Jesus to go through what he did?

What does His experience prove to me?

OT (Isaiah 5) This is prophesy about Jesus and how He becomes our Redeemer, our Messiah.

NT (John 4:25-27) [25] The woman said to him, "I know that Messiah is coming (he who is called Christ). When he comes, he will tell us all things." [26] Jesus said to her, "I who speak to you am he."

Meat and Potatoes

[He Does Not Want to Do It Again!]

I thanked Jesus for what He has done for us and told Him I love Him. This is our conversation:

I don't know how you were able to go through what You went through for us.

It was love that made it possible; unconditional, sacrificial love.

You are love.

Yes. It is who we are, pure love.

It was not at all what the paintings show, was it?

No, not at all. I don't think anyone could paint what I was on that cross . . . All of the world's sin, all the disease, all the hatred, all the fear, all the corruption, all the pain, all the despair, fused onto me . . . not to mention the beating that ripped through skin and muscle and nicked bone. I really did not look human, barely anyway . . . Mmm, I could not do it again.

Abba knows that. [Abba is the Aramaic word for Father.] Once was enough.

I thank Abba for that!

Me too, Lord. I thank You for taking my sin, in my place, and suffering my punishment. There are no words that can ever describe how grateful I am, how grateful all people should be, because You did it for all. The least I can do is to bring more people into Your kingdom, because You sure earned the right to have more people in Your kingdom, over which Father made You King. And the amazing thing is that You're not stuck on power, like most worldly kings or rulers, but on us bringing more people into Your kingdom so they can live and prosper in freedom and love and blessings, like we do. You are truly amazing.

(Father God spoke up.) I agree. But all you humans are amazing as well.

Yes, because You see us as You created us to be. I wish we all could see ourselves as You see us.

I wish that as well, because it is who you really are, not what Satan wants you to believe you are. He is a liar, a deceiver, a destroyer. My Son is the Truth, the Living Word, the Redeemer. He has righted the wrongs, and brings life and light through Holy Spirit, into the world. Satan is the destroyer; Yeshua (Jesus) *is the Savior. I honor him for that.*

Study 2 - Understanding Who God Is

You will never have confidence in God until you understand who

He really is.

PAGES (1st) 5-13   (2nd) 4-13

There are three attributes of God that show that God is God. Write down what they mean.

1. Omniscience:

OT (Psalms 139:1-6) David recognized that God knew everything about him; where he was, what he thought, what he said and where he went. He knew God surrounded him. God's knowledge was so deep and vast that David knew he would never achieve God's all-knowing capability.

NT (Hebrews 4:12-13) God discerns the thoughts and intentions of your heart, and nothing is hidden from His sight. He knows everything you think about and do, and some day you will give an account to Him.

2. Omnipotence:

OT (Jeremiah 32:17) Jeremiah recognized that God was the Creator and because of His power nothing was too hard for Him to do.

NT (Matthew 19:25-26) Jesus told His disciples that because of Father God's power, nothing was impossible for Him. He is saying the same to you. If you are living in eternal life as God's child, representing Him, nothing is impossible for you because you have His power and authority, through Holy Spirit.

3. Omnibenevolence:

OT (Psalms 145:9) Because of God's goodness, His mercy is over everything that He created. Unfortunately, His goodness is not seen everywhere because of Satan's influence in the world. God wants to give His mercy to all, it is there, but He gave humans the right of choice, and not everyone accepts that mercy.

NT (Acts 10:34-38) Peter reminds the people that Jesus went about showing God's love and compassion, because God was with Him.

Is God with you? He is if you have made Jesus the Lord of your life. **5.** Are you showing God's love and compassion to others?

6. If you are, write down how you are showing God's love and compassion to others. **7.** If you are not, why?

God explained in the book why He is Supreme God. **8.** What did He say about that? **G.** What does that mean? He told Moses this as well. (Exodus 3:14) God is everything to you; whatever you need Him to be; protector, provider, healer, deliverer, wisdom, comforter, teacher, etc.

The book describes five other attributes of God that show Him as personable. **10.** What are they? God is much more than you were led to believe.

Answer the following questions on what the book says about God's attributes:

11. Do you compromise your principles? **12.** Can people trust that what you say is the truth? **13.** Do you compromise yourself? (You say something one time and something different the next.) **14.** If you answered yes to that question, what do you hope to obtain by doing that or what would others think they would obtain? **15.** Do you realize that people are lying when they do that?

16. What is a lie? You are instructed not to lie. (Colossians 3:9) You are supposed to be living the truth. It is vital to tell the truth, not only because you are supposed to represent God, but because there is a significant consequence if you keep lying and do not repent. Repent means to change your ways, not just to say you repent. (Revelation 21:8) **17.** Where will unrepentant liars spend eternity? You make the choice.

LIE: to utter falsehood with an intention to deceive; an intentional untruth. ("Dictionary.com/Meanings C Definitions of English Words," 2024a)

The book reads that Love is part of God's character, and it is the driving force behind everything that God does. **18.** Is love a part of your character? **1G.** Is it the driving force behind everything you do? It should be if you are living in eternity. Remember, you are supposed to be representing God, showing His unconditional love to others, 'your neighbors.'

20. When you received righteousness from Jesus, what did you actually get? **21.** For what did Jesus trade His righteousness?

You are now holy because you belong to God. He is part of you, as Holy Spirit. You are now a part of His Holy Nation, where everyone is equal. Every person in this nation is part of the Body of Christ, His 'Church,' one body with one head.

(Romans 12:4-5) We are spiritually joined together. Jesus is the head of this body, and you represent His physical body. He is no longer on the earth in physical form, so you must be His arms and legs and voice in this worldly realm. This is the purpose of His Church. (You will cover more of this topic (**22.** When it comes to justice, do you consider that we have fair justice in this world? **23.** If you answered "no" write down what you think the reason is for the injustice in this world.

The book says God's judgement is fair because He has the same standard for everyone. **24.** What is that standard?

God talks about wanting to bless His people, but most blessings are not delivered. That is sad. He mentions one of the reasons for that. **25.** What is it? **26.** Can you think of and list more reasons?

27. What are you to do with all the blessings God has given you? (1 Peter 4:10) **28.** If you do this, what are you doing for people?

Jesus gave up His divinity to become human. (Philippians 2:5-7) **29.** According to the verse, what did He come as, besides human? Then you are to be one as well.

Often God's people do not act like royal children of God. They look like and act like the people of the world; there is hardly any difference. (1 John 2:16) **30.** What does it say is from the world? This is what caused the fall of Adam and Eve.

(Ephesians 5:11) The verse speaks of the works of darkness. **31.**

What are you to do about them?

32. How would you answer this question from the book: If you were arrested for being a Christian, would there be enough evidence to convict you? **33.** Why or why not?

You have no authority over the world if you are not turned on to the Holy Spirit, because it is through Holy Spirit that our authority and power are activated.

In the book, the workings of the Holy Spirit are compared to an electrical circuit. Answer the following questions about this example.

34. Who is the bulb? **35.** Who is the power source? **36.** What represents the Holy Spirit? **37.** What controls the on and off switch? **38.** What represents your spirit? **3G.** How do you receive the power from Holy Spirit to light your bulb?

This means that you stop being influenced by carnal [physical] things and become influenced by Holy Spirit. You are letting Him direct your life and He gives you His power to overcome temptation and to do God's will. Remember, you buried your old carnal way of operating [your old person] and have been risen with Christ, operating in the power of Holy Spirit. [Your new person]

Many of God's people are still trying to live from the old person. We had a conversation about that. (God's words in italics, mine in regular print.)

You are such a cool God. I wish more people knew that.

Me, too. Many of my own people do not know that. It is because they do not have a personal relationship with me. They have never tried to get to know me. How do humans get to know other humans?

By spending time together and talking with each other.

Yes. It needs to be that way with me. (Big sigh) I love them so much, and they are selling themselves short. They could be so much more if they just knew me.

God loves you so much and He misses you, cherishes you, and wants to share in your life because He wants to be the best Father for you. Please let Him.

The things you are learning are the amazing benefits of having a personal, spiritual relationship with God. All these things that you are studying should be giving you a desire to know God better and let Him become your best friend.

THINGS TO THINK ABOUT BEFORE THE NEXT STUDY

How can I become a better friend to God?

OT (Psalm 25:14) The friendship of the LORD is for those who fear him, and he makes known to them his covenant. [Fear, in this regard, means to have reverential awe or respect for God.]

NT (Romans 6:3-14) [3] Do you not know that all of us who have been baptized into Christ Jesus were baptized into his death?

[4] We were buried therefore with him by baptism into death, in order that, just as Christ was raised from the dead by the glory of the Father, we too might walk in newness of life. [5] For if we have been united with him in a death like his, we shall certainly be united with him in a resurrection like his. [6] We know that our old self was crucified with him in order that the body of sin might be brought to nothing, so that we would no longer be enslaved to sin. [7] For one who has died has been set free from sin. [8] Now if we have died with Christ, we believe that we will also live with him. [9] We know that Christ, being raised from the dead, will never die again; death no longer has dominion over him. [10] For the death he died he died to sin, once for all, but the life he lives he lives to God. [11] So you also must consider yourselves dead to sin and alive to God in Christ Jesus. [12] Let not sin therefore reign

in your mortal body; to make you obey its passions. [13] Do not present your members to sin as instruments for unrighteousness but present yourselves to God as those who have been brought from death to life, and your members to God as instruments for righteousness. [14] For sin will have no dominion over you since you are not under law but under grace.

Meat and Potatoes

[A Conversation with Holy Spirit.]

Holy Spirit, do You have anything You want to tell me about Yourself. I know Father and Jesus, but I don't feel like I know You much.

I am the connection between the worldly realm and God's spiritual realm, between death and life. Without me you would stay dead; disconnected from God. I am the Spirit of God that connects to your spirit. That makes life possible for you, or anyone else that chooses life over death; Light over darkness; Good over evil; Holiness over unholiness. When a person accepts Yeshua (Jesus) as Savior and Lord, He gives me to you, or rather, He exchanges me for your sins. He did that over two thousand years ago. So, when you invite Jesus into your heart, I come right over to you. I am God's voice, and I am also the connection between your mind and our mind, between your imagination and our imagination.

What if people don't have you in their hearts? Are their minds and imaginations connected to Satan's?

Only if they give Satan permission, by believing the thoughts he puts in their minds, which are lies. Remember, Satan has no authority of his own. The only way he has any authority is if humans give him theirs. If people decide to take back what Jesus redeemed, their authority, Satan would lose control of that person because they have accepted Jesus as their Redeemer. When He suffered, died, and rose again, He broke the chokehold Satan had over the world. We won! Satan lost. A person must reclaim that authority; however, they can only do that if they have the power to wrest it from Satan.

But they don't have control, so they don't have the power.

That is correct. Satan has all their power.

Hmmm. . . Then how . . . Oh! They get the power from You!

Yes. They accept Jesus and I come into them. I am the connection to God's power. Now they have power to get their authority back, because Satan must comply because we won, he lost. People give Satan too much credit. They think he is all-powerful, a god so to speak. Well, that is what he wants. He wants to be like God, but he isn't, humans are. You are the ones made in our image, and if you have accepted Yeshua as Savior and Lord, you become one with us. Satan is very jealous of you humans.

Study 3 - Truths That Must Be Understood

Truth gives you the ability to make good decisions because you are enabled to figure out the difference between carnal things and spiritual things, which means you can discern Satan's lies. Truth is what sets you free from the influence of Satan and the constraints of the world.

PAGES (1st)14-23   (2nd) 14-23

1. List the three truths that you should understand before you can commit to a lasting relationship with God.

2. What does the given scripture say faith is?

You have heard the term "Let my will be done on earth as it is in heaven." You must activate your spiritual senses and have faith in what God has said in His Word. Then you voice that truth aloud so that what God has already done in heaven, the spiritual realm, can manifest into the physical realm. This is what it means to let God's will be done on earth as it is in heaven.

3. Where does the book say faith comes from? (Ephesians 6:16)
4. What is the purpose of the shield of faith according to this verse? Your faith is the shield that destroys Satan's attacks. Faith in God's Truth is your defense against Satan's lies because he has no defense against God's Truth.

5. Why did Jesus have to be the Redeemer? **6.** How did Adam sin?

7. What does carnal mean?

The book talks about God's manifest presence and sin, and about Adam and Eve's life after God kicked them out of the Garden of Eden. The following four questions deal with those topics.

8. Why did God have to remove His Spirit from Adam and Eve when they sinned? **9.** How was Adam and Eve able to function in the world after God had removed His Holy Spirit from them? **10.** According to God, what is death? **11.** Explain why your personal relationship with God must be spiritual.

God talks about how your physical body and your spirit are linked. (John 11:38-44) **12.** How long had Lazarus been dead before Jesus arrived at the tomb?

This is significant because the Pharisees knew it may be possible for God to raise up a dead person, but only up to three days after they died. They thought that a spirit could linger for that long. They did not believe that someone could be raised up after that because the spirit would have left by then and the body would have been in a greater decomposition state, and it would stink! Jesus waited more than three days to raise Lazarus, so that people would know that he was who he said he was: The Son of God.

Here is something to think about: Jesus had to call Lazarus by name when He told him to come out. If Jesus had not done that, then everyone in the tomb would have come out.

Lazarus's spirit had left his body, so it started to decompose. When Jesus told Lazarus to come out, his spirit reentered his body, overriding the decomposition. Your spirit and your body are two separate things but are dependent on each other. A spirit does not need a body to exist, but a body needs a spirit to exist. However, the spirit needs the body to be able to interact in the world. Remember, the body is an "earth suit."

13. What is the key to your spirit having authority over your body?

14. God says you are not a mere mortal because you are His child, what does that entail?

Adam and Eve lived in eternity with God when they were in the Garden of Eden, and they walked and talked together. They had a wonderful spiritual relationship, enjoying their friendship, and everything was perfect; there was no death or fear.

(Genesis 3:8) **15.** What did Adam and Eve do after they sinned?

16. What happened to Adam and Eve after they sinned?

[Note: In the first edition of WAKE UP CHURCH! it talks about time. Time gave Adam and Eve a chance to repent. However, time already existed in the world, because where there is matter there is also space and time.]

(Look at Genesis 1:1) In the beginning, (time) God created the heavens (space) and the earth (matter).

Adam and Eve lived on the earth, but they were not affected by time because they lived from their spiritual person in eternity. When they sinned, they lost their connection to the spiritual realm when they lost Holy Spirit, and they fell into a timeline. This was not well defined in the first edition. This was revised in the second edition. Here is what is written in the second edition:

When Adam and Eve sinned, they fell into a timeline. They lost their connection to God in the spiritual realm. In the physical realm, time is needed so things do not all happen at the same time. Time gave Adam and Eve a chance for redemption. If they had not fallen into a timeline, they would have immediately died with no chance of repenting. Death is the consequence of sin. (Remember, death is eternal separation from God.)

17. According to the book, why are you not bound by time when you operate from the spiritual mind? You do not have to wait to go to heaven to get your blessings, you can have them now. You are not conformed to this world when you live in the eternal realm.

This means you do not have to sin. Your relationship with God helps you see sin as sin and not just as a normal part of daily life.

18. What does "We need to let go and let God" mean to you personally? Anything that does not belong to God is unholy. The original Hebrew word "qudosh" and the original Greek word "hagios" means "to be set apart, sacred, and sanctified."

(Leviticus 20:26) **19.** Why has God separated you from the world? That means you are His child.

20. According to the book, when are you being unholy? You must be clean so that others can see a difference between your life and theirs. (2 Corinthians 7:1) **21.** Since you have these promises, what should you do? This means that our holiness is completed in our reverential awe or respect of God. Without holiness no one will see the Lord. (Hebrews 12:14) **22.** What two things are you to strive for?

For you to bring someone else into God's kingdom, you must be holy. If not, they will not see the Lord because you have not been the example to them that you are supposed to be. *Remember: set apart, sacred, and sanctified.*

SET APART: separate something [you] **and keep it for a special purpose.** [Doing God's will] (Oxford Learner's Dictionaries/Find

Definitions, Translations, and Grammar Explanations at Oxford Learner's Dictionaries, n.d.-b)

SACRED: connected with God [You connected with God through Holy Spirit.] (Merriam-Webster, n.d.-b)

SANCTIFIED: free from sin; purify [Jesus freed you from sin, now purify, (cleanse) yourself by living a holy life.]

This means you mature in your faith, becoming more and more like Jesus. (Merriam-Webster, n.d.-b)

23. When will you not be able to be who God created you to be, and do what you were created to do? You cannot make a difference in the world if you are living worldly; because you cannot do God's will unless you are living spiritually, living holy.

(Ephesians 4:22-24) **24.** What does verse 22 tell you to do? **25.**

What do you think that means?

According to verse 24, you are to put on your new self, because that is how you were created in His image. However, if you are living in unrighteousness and unholiness, you are not operating in His likeness, but in Satan's likeness.

THINGS TO THINK ABOUT BEFORE THE NEXT STUDY

What unholy things in my life are keeping me from being the whole person God created me to be and doing all that He created me to do?

OT (Isaiah 29:13) And the Lord said: "Because this people draw near with their mouth and honor me with their lips, while their hearts are far from me, and their fear of me is a commandment taught by men . . .

NT (Luke 6:46-49) [46] "Why do you call me 'Lord, Lord,' and not do what I tell you? [47] Everyone who comes to me and hears my words and does them, I will show you what he is like: [48] he is like a man building a house, who dug deep and laid the foundation on the rock. And when a flood arose, the stream broke against that house and could not shake it, because it had been well built.

[49] But the one who hears and does not do them is like a man who built a house on the ground without a foundation. When the stream broke against it, immediately it fell, and the ruin of that house was great.

Meat and Potatoes

(Holiness and Unholiness)

When my people mess up, it is imperative for them to get back on track as soon as possible. There is so much to accomplish before Yeshua comes back again. My people cannot do what they need to do as long as they are walking in unholiness. They must get back into my holiness. Constantly search yourself for any unholiness and repent as soon as you realize you are walking in it. Do not give your enemy time to get into your mind; cast him out and repent. The longer you stay in unholiness, the more susceptible you are to Satan's influence. Do not give him a chance to get his foot in the door, slam that door shut and lock it. I have given you the keys of my kingdom to do that, use them.

I have given every person that is following Satan's agenda a chance to repent. I love them. I do not want them to spend eternity without me. Unfortunately, many chose to ignore that chance, and so they will suffer the consequences. I must honor their choice because I gave people free will. It breaks my heart, but those that have not repented will be removed or destroyed. Many will die.

I am restoring what has been taken away from my people and from the people of the world who have suffered because of evilness. I am showing people my Love, power, and graciousness. The world will know that I AM God Almighty! But, because I am restoring justice and righting the wrongs, they will also see that I AM God the Compassionate.

All will see that there is nothing that is too big for me to handle. So go out, my people, and be my arms, legs, and voice so that the people of the world will know that I love them and can handle any lousy thing in their lives. Help them see the Truth so they can stop listening to Satan's lies.

I LOVE YOU WORLD!

Study 4 – What We Need to Do

God wants a personal relationship with you. This study covers what you can do to have a relationship with Him.

PAGES (1st) 24-32   (2nd) 24-32

1. In conversations, have you ever referred to God as the man upstairs? **2.** If so, why did you respond that way? Or if not, why would others respond that way?

3. Do you believe that you have a personal relationship with God?

4. When you say, or others say, "the man upstairs" to someone, do you think that person believes there is a personal relationship there? **5.** Why or why not?

It says that you became a friend to God when you accepted Jesus as your savior. (Romans 5:10). Reconcile means to restore friendship with. **6.** How were you reconciled to God?

The following are questions and statements based on the book about how you can develop a best friend relationship with God.

7. What are five things to do to make that happen?

The book lists seven reasons why people may be holding on to things in their lives that are unholy. **8.** Write down the ones that may apply to you. Do not hold back. If you cannot be honest with yourself, you cannot have an honest relationship with God.

When you take the time to honestly examine yourself and truly repent of the unholy things in your life, you are using discernment.

9. What does the book say discernment is?

The true nature of things comes from the spiritual realm, not the

worldly realm which is influenced by Satan who is the deceiver.

(2 Thessalonians 2:9-10) **10.** According to the verse, why are people perishing? **11.** What happens when you "switch off" the Holy Spirit's power?

Reading the conversation with Jesus, you can see that Jesus has a wonderful sense of humor. The more you develop your relationship with Him the more you recognize His humor. Remember, you are made in His image, not the other way around.

12. When you humble yourself, what are you giving up?

SELF-CENTEREDNESS: a single-minded focus on oneself and one's own needs, desires, preferences, and problems. (Find Definitions C Meanings of Words/Britannica Dictionaries, n.d.)

(Philippians 2:3-4) **13.** This verse says not to just look at your own interests, but to do what? **14.** Do you find it hard to humble yourself? (Proverbs 11:2) **15.** What does the verse say comes to a person who is not humble?

When you co not humble yourself, you are leaning on your own understanding instead of God's understanding. There is a high possibility that you will end up in trouble, because you cannot see the big picture. God sees everything. When you are humble, God can give you wisdom so that you make good decisions.

(Proverbs 3:5-7) **16.** What does the verse say God will do if you acknowledge Him in all your ways? **17.** This verse mentions that you should not be what?

Lack of humbleness is really a pride issue, remember what can happen. (Proverbs 16:18) **18.** What does the verse say can happen to a prideful person?

19. According to 2 Chronicles 7:14, what are the reasons that our countries are in such turmoil? **20.** If God's people would do all those things, what would happen?

(Jeremiah 15:19) **21.** What is the last sentence of that verse? This means that when you speak God's words, people turn to you as His representative, but you will not act like they do. They will recognize something different about you. Repentance leads to restoration and restoration leads to the service of God. Remember that you are to do God's will and serve Him by serving others, as this is your purpose as a disciple of Jesus.

What were you taught when it comes to praying? Prayer is not vain repetition: **VAIN - producing no results; useless.** (Find Definitions C Meanings of Words/Britannica Dictionary, n.d.-b)

REPETITION - the action of repeating something that has already been said. (Merriam-Webster, n.d, -b)

What do you think is wrong with saying "God is great, God is good, let us thank Him for our food." at every meal?

According to the book, what is prayer?

Repeating the same prayer every time you pray is not really talking to God, it is just speaking words that you have memorized and becomes insincere. Such as the following shows:

Thursday November 24

Happy Thanksgiving, God. It's kind of sad.

What is?

How we've reduced Thanksgiving to a federal Holliday.

Hmm.

It's a time of celebration, which is fine, but what are we celebrating? A day off from work (which we may get paid for), a day we meet family and friends, gorge ourselves with food, and then sit and watch football or take a nap? Oh, we'll probably say a prayer before we eat: "God is great. God is good. Let us thank Him for our food." Words. We give you words.

Where is our gratitude? Where is that sincere, heartfelt gratitude for Your unending Love and Compassion, for all the provision and protection, for never giving up on us, even when we've strayed from you.

Where is that down-on-our-knees, honest gratefulness to Jesus for paying the penalty for our sins, for making it possible to be with You again? Where is our gratitude for You pulling us up out of the muck when we fall, or to keep us from falling when we stumble?

Where is our gratefulness for the times in our lives when You showed us a way out of situations that seemed utterly hopeless to us?

Instead, it's come to this: "GodisgreatGodisgoodlet usthankHimforourfoodamen." Wait, slow down. What?

"God is great."

Yes, He is. "God is good." Yes, He is.

"Let us thank Him for our food." Okay . . . Go ahead.

"What?" Go ahead.

"Uh. . . we already are. Pass the mashed potatoes, please."

- PS Welsh

The book says not to wait to do something that God is telling you to do. **25.** Why is that? **26.** Have you ever waited to do something, or not even done something that God told you to do? **27.** Why?

To be an effective disciple of Jesus, we must be willing to do or go when God tells us to do so, this is what His Remnant does. The Remnant is the group of disciples of God that put their faith into action, it is a lifestyle for them. It is His Ekklesia. (More on that later.)

This is why that personal relationship with God is so important. You will begin to hear Him more as your friendship grows and you will begin to trust Him more as well. This will increase maturity in your faith in Him, and you will do His will more times than not.

28. What are some other reasons people may wait, or to do nothing that God wants them to do?

Fear is a big reason people do not do what God is telling them to do. **29.** What fears might you have?

Take heart. In the Bible, according to some, it talks about not fearing 365 times, which equals one per day.

(Isaiah 12:2) Let yourself trust in God. Trust like David did. (Psalms 28:7-9) **30.** What is David doing with the song he is singing in this verse? In verses 8 and 9 he is praying for you. **31.** What does he ask the Lord to do for you?

Fear happens when you do not trust God, and you cannot trust Him if you do not know Him. This is why that spiritual relationship with Him is so important. Get to know Him and feel His love for you, for it will cast out your fears. (1 John 4:18A)

THINGS TO THINK ABOUT BEFORE THE NEXT STUDY

What can I do to strengthen my relationship with God?

OT (Psalm 63) [1] O God, you are my God; earnestly I seek you; my soul thirsts for you; my flesh faints for you, as in a dry and weary land where there is no water. [2] So I have looked upon you in the sanctuary, beholding your power and glory. [3] Because your steadfast love is better than life, my lips will praise you. [4] So I will bless you as long as I live; in your name I will lift my hands. [5] My soul will be satisfied as with fat and rich food, and my mouth will praise you with joyful lips, [6] when I remember you upon my bed, and meditate on you in the watches of the night; [7] for you have been my help, and in the shadow of your wings I will sing for joy. [8] My soul clings to you; your right hand upholds me. [9] But those who seek to destroy my life shall go down into the depths of the earth; [10] they shall be given over to the power of the sword; they shall be a portion for jackals. [11] But the king shall rejoice in God; all who swear by him shall exult, for the mouths of liars will be stopped.

NT (Matthew 22:37) And he said to him, "You shall love the Lord your God with all your heart and with all your soul and with all your mind.

Meat and Potatoes

[Remnant Member]

Help me be a true member of Your Remnant, Lord.

*Well, you must keep seeking the Truth, but, of course, it is more than that. You must live the Truth, no matter what is going on in the physical realm. Stand up for the Truth! Declare the Truth! And live the Truth! This is what my Remnant does, there is no namby-pambiness. (**NAMBY-PAMBY: lacking in character or substance; weak, indecisive**.) (Merriam-Webster, 2024) There is no compromise, no what-if. They have allowed my Truth to set them free. They live from my Spirit no matter what the world wants. They are willing to die for the Truth, like Shadrach, Meshach, and Abednego. (They were the three men who refused to worship an idol and was thrown into a fiery furnace but was not harmed. They did not even smell like smoke when they came out of the furnace. See Daniel 3)*

Are you willing to die for my Truth?

Yes, Lord, but will that always be true? It does cause me to wonder. Just look at Peter . . .

That is why you need to read and study the Truth every day, so that it becomes a part of who you are, second nature, just like it was for Jesus. Study Him. He is my Word, my Truth. He is the one that gives you the keys to set people free. He does not set them free, my Remnant does, as his representatives. He made it possible by becoming the Redeemer. My Remnant, His Ekklesia is what unlocks the chains of darkness.

Because Your light shows us the way and allows us to see the chains.

Yes, that is correct. You cannot unlock chains if you cannot see them. Holy Spirit gives you that Light. That is why you must have a personal, spiritual relationship with me, and live out my Truth. It must be your lifestyle.

Study 5 - What God Will Do

A relationship is not one sided. When you seek a relationship with God, He will be an active part of your relationship. He wants to assure you of that.

(Matthew 6:25-34) **1.** What does the verse say we cannot add to our lifespan? One of the things God will do when you have a relationship with Him is to take care of you. **2.** He wants to be active in your life and give you the things you need, but what does verse 33 say you are to do for Him so He can bless you with everything you need?

PAGES (1st) 32-44   (2nd) 33-45

These pages explain the six things God will do when you have a relationship with Him. **3.** What are they?

4. In the narrative about the widow, what did God do to show her His personal love for her? He wants your relationship with Him to be eternal, to show His personal love and care for you forever.

(Psalms 16:11) **5.** According to this verse, what does God make known to us? Remember, He said that if you acknowledge Him, he will make your path straight.

One of the most important things God will do is to teach you His Truths. (Proverbs 30:5) **6.** Why does God's Word never fail?

7. According to the book, why is God happy to show you His Truth?

8. Why is God not happy with the leadership of His Church? Of course that does not apply to every leader, but it does apply to many. [More on that later]

When teaching you, God will have you practice what you are learning, because you cannot learn everything all at once. Remember: milk, soft food, meat. He teaches you what you can learn based on your level of maturity. It is up to you to press in and study the Truth He has given you to mature.

Put into practice what you are learning. People make excuses so they do not have to do what God is showing them. When that happens, God's will is not being done, and that is not a good thing. **9.** What are some of the excuses you make? [You are not the only one, we all fall short.]

(2 Timothy 2:15) **10.** As a worker, what should you rightly handle? One of the biggest excuses is, "I can't do that." This may be true, you can't, but Jesus can through you. It is not through your own power, but His power through Holy Spirit that gives you the ability to do what God would have you do, and to live like Jesus did.

(Acts 1:8) **11.** According to the verse, when will you receive power?

The book explains why God can give us spiritual solutions to physical problems. **12.** Why can He do that? Spiritual solutions come from Holy Spirit and are often unexpected.

13. What was the spiritual solution to the physical problem in the narrative about the broken mirror bracket? Notice that the spiritual solution included a physical object. **14.** Why are the worldly solutions usually temporary?

15. What two things should you do if you develop a problem?

The book says that God will empower you. **EMPOWER: give (someone) the authority or power to do something.** (Find Definitions C Meanings of Words/Britannica Dictionary, n.d.) God has things for His children to do. It makes sense that He would give you His authority and empower you to do what needs done. He will never leave you defenseless. However, you are defenseless at times because you turn your switch down to the Holy Spirit's power. **16.** According to the book, what can hinder the Holy Spirit's power?

17. What is your true point of view? **18.** What is the reason God's perspective should be your perspective?

19. According to Acts 1:8, when will you receive power? **20.** In the narrative about the crash, what happened that seemed impossible to do in the physical realm? Nothing is impossible with God.

In the narrative about the camp, it shows Holy Spirit can give a person the ability to influence the course of events. **21.** What real-life situation happened that proves this is true?

22. What did God say about His people that do not live out His Truth? **23.** Why is that? To make a difference in the world, you must have the personal relationship with God. **24.** Why?

Your personal spiritual relationship with God is the most important thing in your life! You need to mature, and it is that relationship which makes that possible.

THINGS TO THINK ABOUT BEFORE THE NEXT STUDY

Think back on your life. Were there times when Holy Spirit may have intervened on your behalf, or through you on someone else's behalf, and you were maybe not aware of it at that time?

Do you know anyone else that may have happened to?

OT (Proverbs 19:21) Many are the plans in the mind of a man, but it is the purpose of the LORD that will stand.

NT (Romans 8:37-39) [37] No, in all these things we are more than conquerors through him who loved us. [38] For I am sure that neither death nor life, nor angels nor rulers, nor things present nor things to come, nor powers, [39] nor height nor depth, nor anything else in all creation, will be able to separate us from the love of God in Christ Jesus our Lord.

Meat and Potatoes

(Trickle Power)

Most of my people have their switches turned to the "trickle" position. That is just enough power to keep the light on, but it is very, very dim. There is not enough power to let my light shine through the darkness. This is what has been going on with my people for ages. It is the reason why the world is in such dire straits. What is the meaning of **"DIRE"? Extremely serious or urgent.** (Merriam-Webster, 2024)

There is not enough time left for trickle power. Every one of my people must have their switches turned up to full power. Time is almost over. Look at the first half of Isaiah 55:6: "Seek the Lord while He may be found. Call upon Him while He is near."

I am still here on earth through my people, but when this world revival is over, I will send Jesus to come back and take our people out of the earth and bring them home. At that point we will not be near to the people on earth, because my temples, my people, have been removed. We will still be available because of what Jesus did on humankind's behalf, but when the people of the earth accept Him as Savior and Lord, it will be as martyrs. Why? Satan will have full control over the world because my people are not there to resist him. If people do not agree to live under his control, then they are worthless to him and his one-world order and they will be executed.

Do you think this is what I want? If my people are not representing me now on earth, then this will happen to people who are left behind. If they want to give their lives to Jesus at some point after that, it will be a very stressful and difficult life until they are caught and executed. I do not want that for anyone. This is why I need my people, now, to wake up, turn up your power switches and show up in the world as my ambassadors, my representatives. I want as many people as possible to enter my kingdom now, so they are not martyred later, or so they do not fall into eternal death without me.

Study 6 - How We Can Learn to Commune with God

It is not easy to learn how to commune with God. You have existed in the carnal realm from the time you were conceived. You have used your physical voice for almost the same amount of time. It is difficult to relate to the spiritual senses, but if you want a spiritual relationship with God, communication is especially important.

PAGES (1st) 45-57   (2nd) 46-58

One at a time, list the 8 things you can do to grow confidence in your ability to commune with God.

1.

Dedicating a specific time each day to calm your mind, let the world go, and listen, is immensely helpful in developing your relationship with God and learning to commune with Him. Make it a part of your normal routine, then you will find peace and rest.

(Matthew 11:28-30) **1a** What does Jesus say about His yoke?

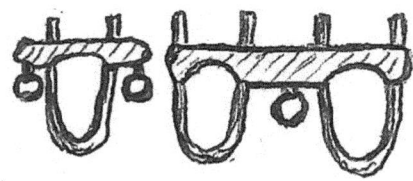 The yoke beam is put on the animal's neck, then the u-shaped bow is inserted up through holes in the beam to secure the yoke to the animal. Cotter pins on each end of the bow hold the bow in place. A wooden shaft, connected to whatever is being pulled, is inserted in each ring, and secured.

Referring to the picture and the scripture mentioned, the single yoke would be what you use to pull the load that you have to bear. It is by your own effort. Jesus said to take His yoke upon you which is a double yoke. **1b** Who do you suppose is carrying the other side of the yoke?

1c Do you see why He says His yoke is easy and light?

You still have the same load to bear, but now it is a lighter load for you, and much easier to pull because Jesus is bearing it with you.

2.

2a According to the book, why is it so hard for you to let go of certain worldly things in your life? Letting go of worldly things that stress you out, and giving God your full attention, even if it is fifteen minutes, will give you a peace that passes all understanding and carries over into the rest of your day.

(Philippians 4:7) **2b** What does this peace do? This peace helps you cope with whatever is going on in your life, because you have hope again. (Romans 15:13) **2c** How are you able to abound in hope?

3.

The book references Colossians 3:2, which says to set your mind on things that are above. In other words, think on spiritual things of God. (1 John 2:17) **3a** Who abides forever?

ABIDE: to dwell, remain, be present, and to be held and kept. (Webster's Dictionary 1828-Online, n.d.) That is a personal relationship with God.

The book says that praising God is very important. (Psalm 22:3)

3b When you praise God what are you doing?

ENTHRONE: to seat in a place associated with a position of

authority or influence; to assign supreme virtue or value to;**exalt** (Merriam-Webster, 2024) When you praise God you are putting Him above everything else in your life, you are worshipping Him. **WORSHIP: to honor or show reverence for, as a divine being or supernatural power; to regard with great or extravagant respect, honor, or devotion.** (Merriam-Webster, 2024) How you live your life should be as worship to God.

(Romans 12:1) **3c** What does the verse say is your spiritual worship to God? This means you are living out the Truth of God; it is your lifestyle. **3d** Are you worshipping God with your life or are you worshipping someone else?

4.

4a Do you let Holy Spirit help and guide you? This is one of the reasons He has come into your life. (John 14:26) **4b** What does Jesus say the Holy Spirit will bring to you?

5.

5a According to the book, why is keeping a journal one of the best things you can do?

5b Do you ever think that you are not worthy for God to bless you? **5c** If so, why? The book says that God thinks you are worthy. **5d** Why?

5e Why does God want people to write down His words? It says that God also communicates with you through visions. **5f** Why are visions effective?

6.

Another way God communicates with you is through your imagination, but many of His people think that imaginations are childish. His response to that: (Matthew 18:2-3) **6a** What must you do to enter the kingdom of heaven?

Children have not squelched their imaginations and limited God. When you ignore your imagination, you could be limiting what the Holy Spirit can do through you.

You must have discernment because Satan also tries to influence people through their imaginations. If you have shut off the power of the Holy Spirit by switching to carnal thinking instead of spiritual thinking, Satan can pollute your imagination, which then becomes vain imaginations, and that is not a good thing. (Genesis 11:1-9) **6b** Why did God confuse the people's language?

God scattered the people, because He knew if all the people could join their imaginations, which had been polluted by Satan, they could accomplish whatever they agreed upon. **6c** What does the book say will happen if you misuse God's gift of imagination?

6d Looking at the gifts Holy Spirit gives to people, write down the ones that you may have had. You may have a gift all the time, but some may be given to you for a particular reason at a particular time, because Holy Spirit gives the gifts as needed. **6e** Are you using the gifts that Holy Spirit gives you to further God's kingdom on earth, or are you using them to further Satan's kingdom or yourself? Remember, you are to represent the kingdom of heaven. This is why you worship God with your life, living out His Truth. It should be a lifestyle.

7.

When you have a relationship with someone and are together, you do not ignore them, you communicate your love and care throughout the day. This is how it should be with your relationship with God, you should pray unceasingly. **7a** In the book, what did God compare that to?

The book talks about an open vision that I had. **7b** What is the difference between a regular vision and an open vision? In the vision, I saw Jesus sitting on a patio chair and drinking coffee. **7c** We never said a word to each other, what did we do?

8.

8a If you keep a journal, what are the benefits of reviewing it now and then? **8b** What were the two things that amazed me when I reread my journal for the first time? **8c** What was reinforced to me when I reread the journal?

Learning to commune with God is critical to you as a child of God, and as a disciple of Jesus. If you do not commit to developing your relationship with God and learning to commune with Him, you will find yourself slipping back to your old ways. You will find yourself getting further and further away from Him, until you begin to doubt Him, doubt His Word, His Truth.

In the book God says this, *"But I will never shut off my love for anyone. Nothing is hopeless, the circumstances can still be made right, because in my spiritual realm there is a solution, a cure, a resolution. The problem is that humankind has forgotten this. With us all things are possible."*

Do not ever forget that. Study God's Word, pray and listen to Holy Spirit so that your relationship with God grows stronger. Do not let yourself wander away from Him, it would be awful, not just for you, but for Him as well.

THINGS TO THINK ABOUT BEFORE THE NEXT STUDY

What are some things I can do to help me commune more with God?

OT (Psalm 3:1-6) [1] O LORD, how many are my foes! Many are rising against me: [2] many are saying of my soul, "There is no salvation for him in God." Selah [3] But you, O LORD, are a shield about me, my glory, and the lifter of my head. [4] I cried aloud to the LORD, and he answered me from his holy hill. Selah [5], I lay down and slept; I woke again, for the LORD sustained me.

[6] I will not be afraid of many thousands of people who have set themselves against me all around.

NT (Romans 12:2) Do not be conformed to this world, but be transformed by the renewal of your mind, that by testing you may discern what is the will of God, what is good, acceptable, and perfect.

Meat and Potatoes

(Praise is the key)

My people are beginning to wake up and pray and declare and take authority over Satan's evil; finally. The Remnant is believing me and not what they see or hear in the world. They are blessing people, fellowshipping with them, meeting their felt needs and letting them know that my kingdom is at hand. No matter how dark it is on earth, they are still taking my Light into the world, with peace and joy in their hearts.

My Remnant is living my Word. They are living out Hebrews 13:16: "And do not forget to do good and to share with others, for with such sacrifices, God is pleased." However, something is lacking.

In the heat of the battle we are fighting, my people are forgetting to praise. Praising is very important. The verse before verse 16, verse 15, says this: "By him, therefore, let us offer the sacrifice of praise to God continually, that is, the fruit of our lips giving thanks to his name." When you praise, you are touching both realms at the same time. When you use your mouth to praise, you are calling forth Abba's presence into the physical realm by the fruit of your lips. (Using physical words, speaking aloud)

*Father's Word says in Psalm 22:3: "Yet you are holy, enthroned on the praises of Israel." (God's people) KJV says inhabits in the praise. Both translations are from the Hebrew word yoshev, (Spillman, 2021) which means to **inhabit, sit, settle, etc.** The word for praise is **halal,** (Strong's Hebrew: 1S84- Shine, n.d.) which means **to shine.** When people say hallelujah, they are saying, "God shine through us. In other words, they are saying, "Let the world see God and not us."*

When you praise us, the world can see our power and light enthroned in you, and that opens a way for our presence to come through you and manifest into the physical situation. It is our presence that brings the supernatural into the natural realm, and then we can actually change the circumstances in the world. We bring eternity into the physical realm, and anything is possible in eternity. Why? It is not subject to physical boundaries and laws. Those "miracles" are just normal in eternity. We are bringing the normal (our will) into the abnormal.

I say "abnormal" because what is in the world is my Father's design and plan that has been corrupted. Our presence corrects that.

Study 7 – Never Abandon the Relationship

Again, your relationship with God is the most important thing in your life, never let it go!

PAGES (1st) 58-62   (2nd) 59-63

1. What are the three reasons the book gives for not abandoning your relationship with God?

The book gives a list of promises from God. **2.** Name three you need the most in your life right now.

Here is another promise from God, another benefit not mentioned in the first edition, that we can experience: Friendship: "No longer do I call you servants, for the servant does not know what the master is doing, but I have called you friends . . ." (John 15:15) When you give your life to Jesus, you become, not just His disciple, but His friend as well, and He cherishes that. **3.** Are you His friend? (John 15:14) **4.** What does this verse say?

Think back on your life. **5.** How many times have you risked losing the benefits of God's blessings by letting carnal things take precedence in your life? Give an example. When you let carnal things take precedence, you have turned your switch off to the Holy Spirit's power and have lost the ability to see things from God's point-of-view. **6.** What did you gain by that or what would anyone gain if they did that?

VULNERABLE: susceptible to physical or emotional attack or harm. (Merriam-Webster, 2024)

7. As a child of God, if you are indeed one, when are you most vulnerable to Satan's attacks?

SUSCEPTIBLE: likely or liable to be influenced or harmed by a particular thing; easily influenced by feelings or emotions; sensitive. (Merriam-Webster, 2024) When you switch to the carnal way of thinking you are using emotions to make decisions. Your emotions become "truth," and you believe what you feel is true. Truth is not based on what you feel but on facts.

FACT: something that has actual existence; an actual occurrence. (Merriam-Webster, 2024) (John 17:17-19) **8.** What does Jesus say is truth when he prayed to Father God about his disciples?

In John 14:6 Jesus says he is the way, the truth, and the life. Jesus lived out God's Truth. He is the Living Word of God. You are called out to live the Truth just like Jesus did. What would Jesus do? You do that. Do not trust in your own truth because Satan has influenced you. Emotions are based on his false reality. Look at God's Word, it is Truth. Truth is what has already been done in heaven, an actual existence, and actual occurrence, in the spiritual realm.

Jesus defeated Satan! He is a loser, a nobody, and has no authority over you or anything else in this world, unless you give him authority over your life. This is what has happened in this world, people have given Satan their authority over their lives and as a result, the world is in a terrible condition. You have the authority, but you cannot use it if you are thinking carnally. **9.** Why is that so?

Your authority is based on God's Truth. You must have your power switch turned on high, so Holy Spirit can guide you into the Truth, which will set you free from Satan's deceitful lies. (John 8:31-32)

10. According to Jesus, when will you know the truth and it will set you free?

11. In the book, what does it say about the Satan influenced evil in the world? 1 Peter 5:8 says that Satan is looking to destroy God's people. **12.** Why would he want to destroy you?

13. What are the three major problems caused by shutting out Holy Spirit and thinking carnally? As a result of shutting out the Holy Spirit, God's will is not being done on earth as it is in heaven, and the condition of the world reflects that. **14.** Book-wise, what does it take for you to change the world?

God's will is that everything be conformed to His divine plan.

15. In what condition are things in that plan? **16.** Why is Satan so determined to destroy God's goodness in the world and pollute it?

17. Who is Satan's biggest target? Get your power and protection back!

THINGS TO THINK ABOUT BEFORE THE NEXT STUDY

If you have a need not covered by God's promises listed in the book, find a promise that does cover the need, by doing an internet search: "What verses talk about [your need]?" Write them down and then declare them out loud every day.

OT (Isaiah 41:10) Fear not, for I am with you; be not dismayed, for I am your God; I will strengthen you, I will help you, I will uphold you with my righteous right hand.

NT (Philippians 4:7) And the peace of God, which surpasses all understanding, will guard your hearts and your minds in Christ Jesus.

Meat and Potatoes

[God wants to bless everyone]

You are welcome to everything I can provide, not just what you need, but things you do not need but would enjoy. I AM a loving God. I love my children and want to bless them, just as I bless you. But I want to bless everyone, and that is why I need you to take my light into the world so others can see my Truth, which will set them free from Satan's lies and deceit. Then they too will become my children, and I can bless them as well.

Bring my kingdom near to them. Show them eternity. Show them Jesus.

Study 8 – Do God's Will (part 1)

Doing God's will is the purpose of your life. You need to spread God's love and power so that His name is proclaimed wherever you go.

PAGES (1st) 62-67   (2nd) 63-68

God's will is why things exist. It is God's will that people help each other by passing His love onto others.

1. How are you able to spread God's love so that His name is proclaimed? God has predestined your purpose. (Psalms 139:16)

2. When was your destiny written down? You are not here by accident. Father God needs you! You are here on this earth right now for a specific reason, at this particular time in history.

3. If you are a true disciple of God and you are doing His will, when will you leave this earth? **4.** Did anyone ever tell you this before? **5.** According to the book, what is God's will? **6.** Why has that been altered on earth?

7. According to Jesus, what was the reason He come down from heaven? **8.** What is God's will for the world according to Jesus? **9.** The book says that this is a sovereign will. What does it determine?

10. How can you know what is God's will?

11. Do you realize that you can talk directly to God? Jesus made that possible for you. When Jesus died, the curtain in the temple, separating the Holy Place from the Holy of Holies, where the Arc of the Covenant was, ripped down the middle, opening the doorway to God's spiritual presence. Jesus became our High

Priest; He is the way. We now can commune directly with God through Holy Spirit.

If you do not believe in Jesus as Redeemer, then you will not be redeemed, which means you will stay unholy and be separated from God for eternity. Read Matthew 7:21 again. Jesus says not everyone who calls Him Lord will get to heaven. **12.** Who does?

(Matthew 7:15-20) The verse says to beware of false prophets. **13.** How will we recognize them? **14.** What do you think Jesus meant when He said good trees bear good fruit, bad trees bear bad fruit?

(Matthew 7:22-23) **15.** What did Jesus say about people who do good deeds, but do not give up their unholy way of living? They never accepted Him as Lord of their lives, which means they did things for their own glory, not God's. Good deeds do not get you to heaven. Living out God's Truth does; living holy.

(1 John 3:1-10) **16.** What is lawlessness? **17.** What does verse 6 say? **18.** According to verse to 10, what are the two things that people do not do, which proves they are not of God?

19. (1 John 5:12) What does this verse say? **20.** Are you a true believer? **21.** Is Jesus truly the Lord of your life? **22.** Is your life a replica of His?

23. Do you have confidence in where you will be spending eternity? If not, you need to develop a personal relationship with God. You need to figure out if you are living righteously (holy), or unrighteously (unholy).

God told me this: *I have equipped you, my people, with everything you need to accomplish your purposes, and I am always with you. Trust that. Trust me and I will give you wisdom to discern the Truth and to use it wisely. Many of you know much of our Truth, but you do not use it wisely. You do not use it to further our kingdom, and many of you use it to further yourselves, not others.* **24.** What unholy things must you let go of in your life?

25. You are learning about God's will. What does the book say about God's permissive will? **26.** According to the book, when you choose to go against God's will, what have you really done?

Listen to what God says about His own people.

Many of you are letting yourselves be deceived by Satan, because you do not have a personal relationship with me. You are still babies in your faith, relying on others to feed you, and since you are using your carnal minds, you are only getting baby food. You must grow up in your faith, however, until you merge your spirit with mine, you will not be able to mature. The Holy Spirit feeds you the meat and potatoes, and this can only be done through your spirit.

My people, you must search out Truth yourselves and stop relying on other people's words or experiences. IT IS TIME TO HAVE YOUR OWN EXPERIENCES WITH ME. You are running out of time! Repent and turn up your switches, so I can teach you the Truth on a personal level. It is time to grow up. I need you. I love you.

THINGS TO THINK ABOUT BEFORE THE NEXT STUDY

In the last year, when have I let go of my relationship with God and made decisions based on my emotions, on my will instead of God's will?

How would things have been different if I had listened to Holy Spirit instead of my feelings?

OT (Isaiah 42:18-20) [18] Hear, you deaf, and look, you blind, that you may see! [19] Who is blind but my servant, or deaf as my messenger whom I send? Who is blind as my dedicated one, or blind as the servant of the LORD? [20] He sees many things but does not observe them; his ears are open, but he does not hear.

NT (1 John 3:16-34) [16] By this we know love, that he laid down his life for us, and we ought to lay down our lives for the brothers.

[17] But if anyone has the world's goods and sees his brother in need, yet closes his heart against him, how does God's love abide in him? [18] Little children, let us not love in word or talk but in deed and in truth. [19] By this we shall know that we are of the truth and reassure our heart before him; [20] for whenever our hearts condemn us, God is greater than our heart, and he knows everything. [21] Beloved, if our heart does not condemn us, we have confidence before God; [22] and whatever we ask we receive from him, because we keep his commandments and do what pleases him. [23] And this is his commandment, that we believe in the name of his Son Jesus Christ and love one another, just as he has commanded us. [24] Whoever keeps his commandments abides in God, and God in him. And by this we know that he abides in us, by the Spirit whom he has given us.

Meat and Potatoes

(Do not give up your divinity)

When I was born, I was just like any other baby, dependent on my earthly parents for everything. I was totally human. The only difference between me and you, when you were born, was the fact that I was born holy, you were not. I had the Holy Spirit, you did not. I had a relationship with Abba, you did not. When I was on earth I felt what you feel, I had needs like you have. I died a physical death like all humans do, unless they were taken up to heaven first.

I was a human just like you are now because you now have Holy Spirit in you. And just like you, I had no power outside of Holy Spirit. I had to commune with Father through Him, we still had a relationship, just as you do, but only through Holy Spirit, just as you do.

Here is the difference between us now. When I died, I suffered a spiritual death and went to hell. I was unholy because I became your sin. If Abba's Spirit had not raised me from the dead, I would still be in hell. When Holy Spirit raised me from the dead, I got my divinity back. That same power that raised me from the dead is inside you, in all my people. When you accepted me as Lord, He raised you from spiritual death, and He can raise others from spiritual death through you.

We are still alike, you and I, both citizens of Heaven and both divine. **DIVINE: of, from, or like God or a god; devoted to god; sacred. It comes from Latin 'divuso' which means Godlike.** (Find Definitions C Meanings of Words/Britannica Dictionaries, n.d.) *When you accepted me, you devoted yourself to us, and became like us, because we are in you and you in us. I am God in physical form. You are like me in physical form. But you are also like us in spiritual form as well. You are Godlike, divine. Do not ever do what I did though. Do not ever give up your divinity, your Godlikeness. Trust me when I say that you DO NOT want to go to hell! The heart-breaking thing is this: some of my people have given up their divinity. They are living from the carnal, not the spiritual, meaning they are no longer living holy. And those that refuse to repent and to live Godlike, have chosen to give up their divinity, just like I did. I chose to give up my divinity, so I could become the Redeemer for all.*

I AM fully God now, not just Godlike when I was on earth. You will never be God, but you have chosen to be Godlike, you have given your life to me, and we are now joined together in Holy Spirit. You are an extension of me, just as I was an extension of Father when I lived on earth. This was why I was able to tell people that when they saw me, they saw the Father. This is why you can say that when people see you, they see me. I guess the question would be, "Do they see me when they see you?" I ask that of all my people, but unfortunately, most would have to say no. They are not like me spiritually.

My purpose was to spiritually redeem people. Meeting their felt needs was a way for me to show them that I cared for them, so that they would give their lives to me. But their spiritual salvation is why I came to earth, which was Father's will. That is what my people should be focused on, not just giving physical things, but bringing my spiritual kingdom to others, by living a lifestyle of Truth.

If you are not addressing the spiritual dimension of poverty in people's lives, which is the result of sin, then you are not completely doing our will. Bringing them into my kingdom is what saves them from death. That is my purpose, and that is your purpose as my representatives.

Study 9 – Do God's Will (part 2)

An effective way of knowing the general will of God is to follow the commandments of Jesus. Remember, Jesus only did Father God's will. He never told us to do what He did not do Himself.

THE FIFTY COMMANDS OF JESUS

(1st) 67-68   (2nd) 68-69

Please read at least one of the listed verses and read the comment or answer the questions in this guide before going to the next one.

OBEY: comply with the command, direction, or request of a person or law; submit to the authority. (Webster's Dictionary 1828-Online, n.d.)

1. If you have made Jesus the Lord of your life, then you should be living under and submitting to His authority. (Ephesians 5:17) What does the verse say about a person who does not take the time to understand what the will of the Lord is?

2. What did Jesus say about a person that hears His words and follows them?

3. (Matthew 4:10) What did Jesus tell Satan to do? Notice that the words worship and serve are in the same verse. We worship God by serving Him. **3a** How do Christians worship someone or something besides God?

4. What does it mean to you to follow Jesus?

5. Salt flavors and preserves. You help preserve God's flavor, His will, His principles, His Word in this world. You are also the light of Jesus in this world or supposed to be. Are you? (Luke 11:35-36) **5a** When will you have no darkness in you? When you turn your switch down to the Holy Spirit, you are turning down His light.

6. (Matthew 5:22) What are you liable to if you call your fellow Christian a fool? We are to respect each other in this body of Christ. In fact, we are to reconcile with each other before giving gifts to God. (Matthew 5:24) **6a** What does Jesus tell you to do before you offer Him gifts?

7. Instant reconciliation means to forgive or be forgiven right away. Why is that so important?

8. LUST: a corrupted desire in a person. (Merriam-Webster, 2024) Every person has desires. Lust is a desire used for unholy purposes; it is a corrupted desire. **CORRUPT: to change from good to bad in morals, manners, or actions; to alter from the original or correct form or version.** (Merriam-Webster, 2024) What corrupted desire do you sometimes struggle with?

When you lust after someone, you have broken a spiritual covenant with your spouse. Covenants are particularly important to God. They are promises in the spiritual realm as well as in the physical realm. A **COVENANT is an unbreakable agreement between two parties that have joined together to support each other.** (What Is a Covenant? Bible Definition and Meaning, n.d.)

(1 Thessalonians 4:1-5) **8a** What should you do with your body? God requires you to be holy which is a part of being a Christian. Holiness belongs to God, so if you are His child, then you are holy. Incidentally, lust cares not about anything but gratifying its own desires, whether it be sex or power, it is self-promoting and self-seeking.

9. Divorcing someone and then remarrying is adultery because a physical covenant was broken, and this covenant was to be for life (Until death do us part). The only cause for divorce in the Bible is for sexual immorality of a spouse (Someone broke the vow, the covenant). Marrying after the death of a spouse is not adultery, the covenant is now void. Why?

10. Oath: A solemn promise, often invoking a divine witness, about one's future action or behavior. (Oxford English Dictionary, n.d.) Who is the divine witness?

(Numbers 30:2) **10a** If you swear an oath to bind yourself by a pledge (promise), what shall you NOT do? **10b.** What SHALL you do? Do not swear an oath because you cannot be 100% sure that what you say is exactly what will occur. You do not know what the future holds. Let your yes be yes and your no be no and mean it. Do not say it if you do not mean it! Remember the divine witness.

11. This commandment is about not retaliating but taking the extra time or step to show God's love to those who mistreat you. Is that hard for you to do? This is a situation where you must call upon the Lord for help because your natural inclination is to revenge yourself. You must approach this from the spiritual realm. Let God handle it. (Romans 12:19) **11a** What should you not do?

12. What does Luke 6:38 say will be measured back to you? (Matthew 6:14-15) **12a** What does this verse say about forgiveness? It even applies to judging others. (Matthew 7:1-2) **12b** What will happen if you pronounce judgement on someone?

13. When you love, bless, and pray, you are representing Jesus, being a "little Christ" to others. When others see God's love at work in you, they are more open to accepting Jesus as their Lord. Why?

14. (Matthew 6:1-4) What is this really talking about?

15. (Matthew 6:5-6) Why did the Pharisees pray long prayers in public? (1 John 2:29) **15a** According to the verse, how do you know you have been born of God? This verse says you need to practice righteous living, not just show off. The Pharisees were looking for accolades from the people. You must humble yourself and live righteously, looking for accolades from Father God. (James 4:10) **15b** What will the Lord do if you humble yourself before Him? **15c** What is the biblical meaning of exalt?

16. Just be sincere and talk to God because that is what prayer is. (Jeremiah 29:11-13) The verse says that when you call upon God and pray to Him, what will happen?

17. Jesus started His prayer with 'Father in Heaven.' (Matthew 6:9) **Pray then like this: "Our Father in heaven hallowed be your name.** Not only are you to pray to Father God, but to pray that His name will be holy and sanctified in your life. **SANCTIFY: to set apart as holy.** (Find Definitions C Meanings of Words/ Britannica Dictionaries, n.d.) Do not do anything that gives God a bad name. In your own words tell why you must have respect for the name of God?

(John 16:23) Here Jesus is referring to the day He would no longer be on earth, and we will have Jesus' authority to act in His name. You are now in that day and now are able to petition God directly through the name of Jesus because you are a follower of His and operate under His authority. **17a** What did Jesus promise you if you would ask Father God for something in Jesus' name? Remember, *in His name* means under His authority. If you are asking something of God that is not something that Jesus would agree with, then you are asking under your own authority, and God does not have to honor that.

(John 16:26-28) Before Jesus left the earth, He would petition God on the disciple's behalf. After He left the earth, they could talk directly to God through the authority of Jesus. Remember, you are Jesus' body, you represent Him and can approach Father God personally because you have Jesus' authority. You approach God in Jesus' name as His follower, and as a child of God, He is grateful for that. This is what He told me:

You have been awesome in this journey with me. I appreciate how you have sought me and now stand on my promises, stepping out in faith, and doing my will, even when you do not understand completely. It will take an eternity to understand it all. Thank you for choosing to spend eternity with me so I can teach you . . . well, forever. I love you my precious child.

THINGS TO THINK ABOUT BEFORE THE NEXT STUDY

When do I make excuses not to follow Jesus and do His will?

OT (Proverbs 19:16) Whoever keeps the commandment keeps his life, he who despises his ways will die.

NT (John 14:15-17) [15] "If you love me, you will keep my commandments. [16] And I will ask the Father, and he will give you another Helper, to be with you forever, [17] even the Spirit of truth, whom the world cannot receive, because it neither sees him nor knows him. You know him, for he dwells with you and will be in you.

Meat and Potatoes

(Sanctification)

I thanked God for talking with me in the mornings and told Him it is a precious time for me. He responded.

Yes, it is. We appreciate this time as well. Not only are you communing with us, but this time is also for sanctification. Look that up.

The verb form is **SANCTIFY: To set apart for special use or purpose, that is, to make holy or sacred. Therefore, sanctification refers to the state or process of being set apart, i.e., "made holy," as a vessel full of the Holy Spirit.** (Find Definitions C Meanings of Words/Brittanica Dictionary, n.d.)

From the time you accept Jesus as Savior and Lord, your sanctification begins, and it is a process that will continue until you leave the earth. Basically, it is the process of becoming increasingly more like Jesus. It is you cooperating with Holy Spirit to help you let go of worldly things and grow stronger in spiritual things; maturing of your faith in my Truth and in what Jesus accomplished for you by his sacrifice and his rising from the dead.

Essentially, it is becoming more like Jesus by believing in him; in how he thought, in what He spoke, in what he did and in how he treated people, and then you doing the same. It is the process of becoming Christlike. It is putting him first in your life, through Holy Spirit, and living out my truth, just as he did. It was not a ritual for him, it was a lifestyle, a way of life. He was living Truth on earth. He is your example. Yeshua was my physical voice, arms, and legs on this earth. He is no longer there physically, you are! Yeshua is the head of his body. He is the spiritual head, the leader, you are his body. You are his physical arms, legs, and voice on earth. If he is the head then you must have his mindset, which directs you, His body.

Do not let anyone else direct his body. When you stop focusing on Holy Spirit and focus on carnal things, you have the mindset of the world, of Satan, instead of having the mindset of Jesus.

You are letting the enemy influence Christ's body. This is very detrimental to you, but also to everyone who sees or hears you. Are you profaning my Son's body? Look that word up.

PROFANE: treat something sacred with irreverence or disrespect. (Merriam-Webster, 2024)

Are you disrespecting my son? Are you disrespecting yourself? Remember, you are now sacred because you are now the body of Christ, the temple of the Holy Spirit. DO NOT LET THE ENEMY INFLUENCE YOU, A PART OF MY SON'S BODY! Get your mind off of carnal things and back on Holy Spirit so he can continue the sanctification process, which is a lifelong thing. If you do not let Holy Spirit sanctify you, you will never be mature enough to accomplish your purpose on this earth. You have an assignment to accomplish. If you had no assignment, I would have brought you home as soon as you accepted Jesus as Lord of your life. Let him direct your life, and do his will, which is my will. Live in obedience to my will so that we can spend eternity together. Remember: one mind, one body with many members.

Study 10 – Do God's Will (part 3)

This study is a continuation of the Fifty Commandments of Jesus. Remember that His commands are what He did Himself.

PAGES (1st) 68-69   (2nd) 69-71

18. According to Matthew 6:25-26, why should you not be anxious?

19. (Matthew 6:19-21) What does it mean when the verse says that where your treasure is, so will your heart be? **19a** Are you focused on the carnal r]V.ealm or the spiritual realm? Your treasure is stored in one or the other place. When God blesses you with physical blessings, do not be greedy, use them to help and bless others. When you do, you are building up treasures in heaven.

20. (John 7:24) How are you to judge? Do not look at the situation from your carnal perspective, but from God's perspective.

21. (Matthew 7:7-11) What does the verse say about those who ask, seek and knock? These verses show you that God is a good God and He wants to bless you beyond measure. He wants you to keep seeking His blessings. **21a** Name some blessings God has given you.

22. This is known as the Golden Rule. How do you think the world would be if everyone just followed this one rule?

23. This ensures that the things of God are kept holy. Arguments can turn unholy very quickly. Can you think of a situation where you or someone else was speaking about something of God and an argument happened? **23a** What was the outcome?

24. There are many verses that talk about forgiveness. (Matthew 18:21-35) The king forgave the servant's debt, so why did the king have the servant thrown into debtors' prison later?

Forgiveness is also important for your future. If you do not forgive, you will always be looking back and will not be able to move forward, which means that you cannot do God's will. Remember what Jesus said about not doing Father God's will. **24a** What did He say?

25. Let the dead in spirit bury the dead, you focus on life. Jesus is saying to put Him first because He is life. In Jesus' time, people would say, "Let me wait to bury someone." In other words, wait until my father dies and is buried then I will follow you. It was the man's excuse not to follow Jesus at that time. (1 Peter 4:6) Who are the dead in spirit?

26. This never made sense to me, because on the one hand it says to fear God, but on the other hand it says not to fear God. A couple of our conversations dealt with this topic, and I am going to refer you to one of those conversations and what God told me. We were talking about fear in a scenario as if I did not know God.

READ PAGES (1st) 151 (2nd) 152 (starting with the definition of fear) and ending with the first three paragraphs of page (1st)**153 (2nd) all of 153 and the first 2 lines of 154.**

If we have made Jesus the Lord of our lives, we should not be afraid of God, but what should we do? There are two perspectives of this command of Jesus. Look at Matthew 10:28. "And do not fear those who kill the body but cannot kill the soul. Rather, fear him who can destroy both soul and body in hell." Someone who has not accepted Jesus as Savior and Lord, will fear people who can kill the body, because if they should die a physical death, they will spend eternity in hell. They have not been redeemed. They are afraid to die because they do not know the Savior and say they do not believe in God. However, the unsaved will be judged by Him at some point and will be cast out of God's presence forever. They should be very afraid, because God can determine who has not made Jesus the Lord of their lives.

Pay attention who Jesus is talking to in this verse. He is talking to His followers, who believe that they will spend eternity with God, so why does Jesus have to remind them not to be afraid of people who can kill the body? Because they are looking at things from the worldly perspective: from fear. They cannot see the truth because they are focused on the worldly things and not on spiritual things that Jesus has told them. Why? They did not have the Holy Spirit's power, because Jesus had not yet become the redeemer.

The Holy Spirit reveals that truth to us today. Unfortunately, most of God's people are still living carnally and so, as a result of our fear, we have not witnessed to people the way we should. Our fear has stopped us from doing our jobs as disciples of Jesus. We forgot the promises of God, because we are not focused on the spiritual things of God. Jesus reminds us that we do not have to fear physical death. All we have to do is fear God. But in this case, fear means to have reverential respect for Him, which means to trust God and give everything over to Him and do His will. We do not have to fear spiritual death because we have eternal life.

Recently God told me this: *Most of my people are sitting back and waiting to go to heaven where they will receive eternal life. You all must realize that you do not make it to heaven if you do not already have eternal life, and that will be determined during the Great Judgement. If you do not live out eternal life on earth by thinking like Jesus, saying what Jesus would say, doing what Jesus would do and treating people the way he would treat them, then you have not made Jesus the Lord of your life. Tragically, he will say to you, "Be gone, I never knew you." Do not* wait to receive eternal life when you get to heaven, it will be too late by then.

Do not let anything or any person in the physical realm keep you from doing my will. Do what Jesus would do. That is living in eternal life.

27. Have you ever been ashamed to talk about what Jesus has done for you? This ties right into number 26. Usually, it is because of fear; fear of what people will think, fear of what could happen, fear of rejection, fear of failing, fear, fear, fear. If you truly understood the unconditional love that God has for you, and the promises that He has given you, you would not be afraid. (1 John 4:18) **27a** Why is there no fear in God's love?

It says fear (being afraid) has to do with punishment. In this case of not doing God's will, it would be punishment of rejection, punishment of government retribution, punishment of less popularity. It is all about conditional love which is self-love and worldly love. Conditional love results in fear. "If I do not meet these conditions, I will not be loved, or respected or held in high esteem, etc. The verse says the one that fears has not been perfected in love. That is because there is only one perfect love and that is God's unconditional love, which comes from the spiritual realm.

If you find yourself doing things out of fear, especially avoiding God's will, you need to understand that you have turned your switch down. You are existing in the carnal realm, not living in the spiritual realm. You are leaning on your own understanding, which is influenced by Satan, and not on God's understanding through Holy Spirit. (Proverbs 3:5-8) **27b** How much should you trust in the Lord?

If you respect God and do his will, you have nothing to fear. You need to develop your personal relationship with God, for truly is the most important thing in your life!!

28. What do you think "take up your cross" means? Refer to number 27. You do what God's will is for you, despite people who will reject you, being less popular, making someone mad, standing up for the truth, and being arrested, being called crazy, just like Jesus took up His cross, on your behalf, even though He did not want to go through what He was going to go through. Remember, He sweated blood. However, Jesus knew that Father God had a special purpose to fulfill through His sacrifice, so He chose to do Father God's will. You need to know that you have a special purpose to fulfill, so you need to choose to take up your cross and do Father God's will as well.

(Mark 8:34-38) **28a** Who will the Son of Man be ashamed of when He comes in the glory of his Father?

THINGS TO THINK ABOUT BEFORE THE NEXT STUDY

Do I love Jesus enough to obey His commandments? What are your thoughts about that?

OT (Deuteronomy 7:9) Know therefore that the LORD your God is God, the faithful God who keeps covenant and steadfast love with those who love him and keep his commandments, to a thousand generations, NT (John 14:15-24) [15] "If you love me, you will keep my commandments. [16] And I will ask the Father, and he will give you another Helper, to be with you forever, [17] even the Spirit of truth, whom the world cannot receive, because it neither sees him nor knows him. You know him, for he dwells with you and will be in you. [18] "I will not leave you as orphans; I will come to you. [19] Yet a little while and the world will see me no more, but you will see me. Because I live, you also will live. [20] In that day you will know that I am in my Father, and you in me, and I in you.

[21] Whoever has my commandments and keeps them, he it is who loves me. And he who loves me will be loved by my Father, and I will love him and manifest myself to him." [22] Judas (not Iscariot) said to him, "Lord, how is it that you will manifest yourself to us, and not to the world?" [23] Jesus answered him, "If anyone loves me, he will keep my word, and my Father will love him, and we will come to him and make our home with him. [24] Whoever does not love me does not keep my words. And the word that you hear is not mine but the Father's who sent me.

Meat and Potatoes

(Wherever you go, He goes)

I realize that when I do not follow God's commandments, I've slipped back into my old ways of thinking, which causes me to do, think or say things that Jesus would not appreciate.

I was singing to God, and the last stanza is "Take joy, my Lord in what you hear, may it be a sweet, sweet sound in your ear." His reply was this:

Always. It is always a sweet sound when you sing. I always hear my people; huh, even when they voice not so sweet sounds. I hear everything a person says or thinks. I am in you. I know what you think because I am spirit. I go where you go, and I see what you see, but I also see what you do not see. There are places I do not want you to go, maybe not because of what you will see, but because of what you cannot see. To you it may look fine, safe or appealing, but it is dangerous, ugly, or evil. I love you. I want to protect you. My commandments, my will is not to lord it over you, but to be your loving Father, to keep you safe, to give you joy and peace. I want you to have abundant life.

Please do not take me where you know I do not want to be. Do not look at what you know I do not want to see. Do not say what you know I do not want to hear. If you do, it could lead to overwhelming fear. I love you and want the best for you. We are one in spirit, so let us go, do, and say together in harmony. When we do, you can see, with me, what you normally cannot see. You are precious to me; you are my child, and I love you beyond measure. I do not just love you for all time, but also for eternity. Time will end, but eternity will not.

I am always with you. Please think about that before you say, do, go, think, or look. We are family. Please respect me as much as I respect you.

Study 11 – Do God's Will (part 4)

We are continuing with the 29th commandment of Jesus.

Pages (1st) 69   (2nd) 70-71

29. HYPOCRISY: the practice of claiming to have moral standards or beliefs to which one's own behavior does not conform; pretense. (Merriam-Webster, n.d.) **PRETENSE: an attempt to make something that is not the case appear true.** (Merriam-Webster, 2024) Do you call yourself a Christian?

The word **Christian** comes from the Greek word χριστιανός (Christianos), **meaning "follower of Christ."** (Christianos Meaning – Greek Lexicon/New Testament (KJV), n.d.) **29a** Are you following Christ? Remember, you are to represent Him in this world. **29b** Are you thinking how He would think? (1 Corinthians 2:16) **29c** What does this verse say about your mind? **29d** Are you saying what Jesus would say?

(Matthew 12:36-37) **29e** How will you be justified on the day of judgement? **29f** How will you be condemned? **29g** Are you doing what Jesus would do? (John 14:12) **29h** What does Jesus say about those who truly believe in Him?

29i Do you treat others the way Jesus would? (Matthew 7:12) **29j** How are you supposed to treat others? Jesus treated people with respect and care. Following Jesus means making Him the Lord of your life. **29k** Is He?

Greed: a selfish and excessive desire for more of something (such as money) than is needed. ("Greed," 2024)

(1 Timothy 6:9-10) It is not money that is the problem, but the love of money is the problem. **29L** Why?

When we focus too much on money and not enough on God, we become selfish and greedy and share less with people who need help. We are to share with others. (Proverbs 3:27) It is a choice. If you choose not to help when you can, it can backfire on you. (Proverbs 21:13) **29n** What is the possible backfire? Keep your life free from the *love* of money. (Hebrews 13:5) Do not let yourself be deceived.

(Galatians 6:7-10) **29n** What does verse 7 say about God? He wants you to have abundant life, but if you mock Him, He will let you reap what you are sowing. That is legal for Him to do because He gave you free will. He is not obligated to protect you from your own foolishness. However, He is obligated to let you make your own choices.

Share, especially with the poor. Jesus told His disciples He came to bring good news to the poor. (Luke 4:18-21) **29o** Besides bringing good news to the poor, what are the four other things that He came to do? Then, so should you.

Jesus was very definite when He talked about His people, His Body. He wants us to treat each other with respect and love, especially if one has done wrong against us. He tells us how to handle the situation so that unity is still possible with the least amount of conflict. (Matthew 18:15-20) What are the three steps to take if a brother or sister in Christ has done you wrong?

30a If it is still not resolved after that, what should be done? (John 13:35) **30b** What is the reason Jesus said that all people will know we are His disciples?

That is what we do not have in today's churches. No, we do not show respect and love to other Christians. We have disharmony because of religion. This denomination doesn't want to have anything to do with that denomination and that church doesn't do things the way another church does, so they won't associate with each other. One church has praise songs and another church sings hymns. People at that church over there wear their best clothes, but that other church, whoo, the people there wear flip flops and shorts! Jesus came to unify us. Did He separate His disciples into groups according to religion, social status, economics, race, gender, or values? NO!

His Ekklesia was open to every single person, and those that accepted Him as Lord of their lives became a part of His kingdom, and they were all equal, and equally important and loved by Jesus. Religion has broken up the body of Christ, and now we have many bodies, each with their own head. People, ONE BODY, ONE HEAD! It is time to come out from behind the church walls and work together with other churches, groups, and peoples, in a concerted effort to fight our real enemy Satan and destroy the evil darkness that has overcome this world! We are supposed to be God's light in this world, but because we do not work together in harmony, we actually push people deeper into the darkness! No wonder God is frustrated. He looks back at what Jesus, His beloved Son, went through for us, for all people, and we, His own, are pushing people deeper into the darkness! Why would He even care about us anymore? Because He loves us all and honors the sacrifice that Jesus made on our, everyone's behalf.

The things of Caesar was money for taxes. The government needs money to function. Unfortunately, they get greedy sometimes but go by whatever the law says until the law is changed. What is really being talked about here are carnal things, worldly things. However, if you are a follower of Jesus then you are Father God's child. You and everything you have, including physical things, is God's. Let him direct you in all things, including money.

Remember these greatest and second greatest commands.

Make sure you are doing the Master's will. (Matthew 7:21) God mentions this verse often.

Refer to 31. You are a child of God.

You should minister to others as you would to Jesus. Would you treat Jesus differently then you treat others?

Commandment 35 said you should minister to people meeting their felt needs. This one says to do it for the purpose of making new disciples of Jesus, teaching them His commandments, and letting them know how important it is to obey those commands. Do not just speak to people, but let your life be an example to them of how they should live. (Matthew 28:18-20) What authority does Jesus have? **36a** What are you to do with the authority He has given to you?

THINGS TO THINK ABOUT BEFORE THE NEXT STUDY

In what ways do I treat other Christians different than I would treat Jesus? Do I treat them differently than Jesus would treat them?

OT (Isaiah 40:3-4) [3] A voice cries: In the wilderness prepare the way of the LORD ; make straight in the desert a highway for our God; [4] Every valley shall be lifted up, and every mountain and hill be made low; the uneven ground shall become level, and the rough places a plain.

NT (Mark 16:14–2014] Afterward he appeared to the eleven themselves as they were reclining at table, and he rebuked them for their unbelief and hardness of heart, because they had not believed those who saw him after he had risen. [15] And he said to them, "Go into all the world and proclaim the gospel to the whole creation. [16] Whoever believes and is baptized will be saved, but whoever does not believe will be condemned. [17] And these signs will accompany those who believe: in my name they will cast out demons; they will speak in new tongues; [18] they will pick up serpents with their hands; and if they drink any deadly poison, it will not hurt them; they will lay their hands on the sick, and they will recover." [19] So then the Lord Jesus, after he had spoken to them, was taken up into heaven and sat down at the right hand of God. [20] And they went out and preached everywhere, while the Lord worked with them and confirmed the message by accompanying signs.

Meat and Potatoes

(Preparing the Way)

You, my Ekklesia, help prepare the hearts of the people for my entrance into their lives. It is so important for their salvation. This is why your faith must be an active faith. Do what I instructed my disciples to do: Bless people, fellowship with them, meet their felt needs and tell them that my Kingdom is near. When you do these things you are helping them straighten out their lives, you are raising them up from the valley of despair and you are giving them hope by allowing them to see the truth concerning that mountain of troubles they have. With me it is just an ant hill.

Study 12 – Do God's Will (part 5)

This study is a continuation of the Fifty Commandments of Jesus. Remember that His commandments are what He did Himself.

PAGES (1st) 69-70   (2nd) 71-72

37. (1 John 5:1-5) Who is it that overcomes the world?

37a (Luke 15:10) What causes the joyfulness of the angels? Jesus even told a parable about a celebration that is held when someone repents and returns to God. (Luke 15:11-32)

You may stray from God. You may live unholy and spiral down into ruin with depression and regret, but your Heavenly Father still loves you and wants you back, because you are precious to Him. It does not matter if you feel completely unworthy; if you repent and turn back to Him, He will run to you and embrace you in his love.

38. Jesus tells us to believe in Him, and Father God also says to believe in Him. (John 3:16) God also says to listen to Him. (Luke 9:28-35) In what form did God's Shekinah presence manifest itself when He said this?

39. In Matthew 18 Jesus tells the disciples that unless someone has childlike faith, they will not enter the kingdom of God. (Matthew 18:2-4) Who is the greatest in the kingdom of heaven? **39a** What do you think it means to have childlike faith?

40. The priests allowed money changers and venders to sell animals to the people for sacrifices and set unreasonable prices for them. (Matthew 21:12-13) Jesus reminded them that God's house was to be a house of prayer for all nations and threw the venders out of the temple court. What did He accuse the venders of?

41. Say what?! Rejoice? (Luke 6:22-23) Why does the verse say to rejoice? Other scriptures offer other reasons to rejoice. (Romans 5:1-5) **41a** What does suffering produce? **41b** What does endurance produce? **41c** What does character produce?

Hope allows us not to be ashamed to stand up and think, say, do, and treat people the way Jesus did. Hope is believing in something that has not yet happened. If you are persecuted for being a follower of Jesus, then you are doing something right. That means that Satan is not happy. You are making a difference!

42. Do not let yourself get too busy or too preoccupied to hear God's word. What are some things that may distract you from hearing God's words?

43. Be the Good Samaritan. The Jews shunned the Samaritans because they had intermarried with non-Jews, and of course the children were considered half-breeds. They were considered impure and heretics. It was a hated Samaritan that helped the Jewish man who was attacked, after being passed by a priest and a Levite, which were part of the religious officials.

This story is actually a parable about the kingdom of God. The priest, who was born into the office, from generation to generation, represents the Law (the old covenant), the Levite represents the prophets (who prophesied about the Messiah). John the Baptist was the son of a Levitical priest, but he became a prophet instead of a priest. The Samaritan represents Jesus, the Messiah, who brings about the new covenant of Grace. He lets His disciples know that it is not just about following laws and rituals anymore, but being reborn in the Spirit, adopted into God's family, and showing God's love to others, no matter who they are or where they are from. Are you being a Good Samaritan?

44. When you respect lowly people, you are showing them that in Jesus' kingdom they are equals with everyone else. (Galatians 3:26-28) What does it say about all these different people? The lowly cannot pay you back, but God will.

45. Humbleness is critical for the Christian, for you cannot put Jesus first if you are not humble. **HUMBLE: not proud or haughty: not arrogant or assertive.** (Merriam-Wester, 2024) (Proverbs 11:2) What comes with the humble?

You need Jesus to be your Lord, first in your life, if you call yourself a Christian. You are not following Jesus if you have not made Him Lord of your life. If you are not following Jesus, you are not a Christian. (Refer to command 29)

46. Your Christian life starts there. When you give your life to Jesus, you receive the Holy Spirit and He gives you spiritual life. From that point forward, you should be influenced and guided by Holy Spirit in every aspect of your life. You are a new person in Christ. Write down how your life is different now. If it isn't different, seriously answer yourself, "Why?" **46a** If your life is not different, then you are not a new person. What can you do to change that?

47. (John 15:1-11) Jesus says that He is the vine, and you are a branch of that vine if you are a child of God. Who is the vine dresser, the one who prunes the branches? It says that you should bear good fruit as a branch in this vine. Read (Galatians 5:22-24) **47a** List that fruit.

These fruits are the characteristics of Jesus. **47b** When someone looks at you, the branch, do they see these fruits, these characteristics in you?

47c Which characteristics are missing in you? Strengthen your relationship with the Lord. The closer you get to Him; the more people will see His characteristics in you. Your life should be representing Him. Remember that it is a lifestyle.

48. (Luke 12:16-21) What did God call the man in this parable? This is a parable about what not to do when it comes to physical wealth. Do not get greedy. You must be rich in God. You do not need to covet anyone else's blessings. (Luke 12:22-31) **48a** What does it say that you should not do?

49. It says to read Mathew 29:19. There is no chapter 29. It is (Matthew 28:19-20) What does Jesus tell His disciples to do? The physical baptism is a sign of repentance and turning away from the old ways. (Acts 19:2-6) **49a** What did John tell the people to do?

Physical baptism signifies you have buried, given up, your worldly way of operating and rising with Jesus in a spiritual baptizing of the Holy Spirit. It is the power of the Holy Spirit that gives you the ability to think like Jesus, speak like Jesus, do like Jesus, and treat people like Jesus did.

50. (Matthew 5:48) Wow. Does this seem impossible to you? The Greek word for perfect is τέλειος. It is an adjective made after the noun τέλος which means the idea of an end-goal or purpose. It is not the state of being perfect, but the process toward reaching that goal of perfection. (Strong's Greek: 5046 Τελειος (Τελος) – **Having Reached Its End, Complete, i**.e., Ext. Perfect, n.d.)

So, Matthew 5:48 would read something like this: therefore, you must strive for perfection as your Heavenly Father is perfection.

PERFECTION: 1: The quality or state of being perfect: such as

    a. Freedom from fault or defect: flawlessness

b. Maturity

c. the quality or state of being saintly

2: the act or process of perfecting (Merriam-Webster, 2024)

Notice the word MATURITY. This is what we have been talking about. Look at this from what Jesus' purpose was here on earth. (2 Corinthians 3:12-18) **50a** What does the verse say is happening to those with unveiled faces, which see the glory of the Lord? That means you are maturing, growing, getting closer to that perfection. Alleluia!

Jesus set you free when He gave you His Holy Spirit. (Luke 4:18)

51. Why was Jesus able to do the things He did? Due to the Holy Spirit, He was able to overcome sin. Your desires tempt you, but it is sin that enslaves you, however Jesus set you free because He overcame that sin. You now do not have to sin because the Spirit of the Lord is upon you; you are no longer enslaved by sin.

(Ephesians 4:11-16) **52.** What does the verse say you are to grow up to be? You must mature in your faith because then you will be able to discern what is evil and what is good. The more you mature the more you will be able to discern truth. Holy Spirit teaches you God's Truth, then you will know what truth is not.

SAINTLY: to be a saint which means to be holy. (Merriam-Webster, n.d.) When you are a child of God, you are holy.

53. Have you ever said something like this? "I'm just human, I know I'm going to sin. That's just the way it is." Often, someone will say that when they do not want to admit that what they want to do is Unholy, and do not want to fight against it. Sometimes they will say that God is tempting them; for whatever reason I do not know. GOD WILL NEVER USE UNHOLINESS TO TEMPT YOU! He is incapable of that, He is holy. (James 1:13) Let no one say when he is tempted, "I am being tempted by God," for God cannot be tempted with evil, and he himself tempts no one.

(James 1:14) **54.** So, what is tempting you? There is a lot of confusion regarding this topic. You must understand that sin and temptation to sin are two different things. Everyone in this world has a temptation to sin, even Jesus did. (Matthew 4:1-11)

55. What were the three responses Jesus gave to Satan when he tempted Jesus? [Notice that He quoted scripture to defend Himself against Satan's attacks]

56. What did He tell Satan to do? Jesus spent forty days in the wilderness tempted by Satan, and you are no different in that respect; you are going to be tempted. Jesus was different in one way than all other humans; He did not give in to the temptations. Here is where you should be different now than the world: not giving in to your desires to sin. This is possible because you now have Jesus.

(James 1:15) **57.** What does fully grown sin bring? When you give in to your unholy desires then sin is the result. Carnal minded people will give in to their unholy desires because they are enslaved by sin. Spiritual minded people, who know the Lord, will not give in to their unholy desires because Jesus has set them free from sin. Now, here is some meat and potatoes: A Christian will not sin if they are operating with their spiritual mind, BUT they can sin if they are operating from their carnal mind. **58.** Do you have your switch turned up or down, on or off?

(Romans 6:12-14) **59.** What does verse 14 say? God's Grace has made you a new person in Christ. Instead of saying you are human, you are just going to sin, you should be saying, "Holy Spirit will help me overcome my desire to sin, because Jesus overcame sin." Because you are a child of God, you have authority over sin. You do not have to sin just because you are human.

(James 4:7) "Submit yourselves therefore to God. Resist the devil, and he will flee from you."

THINGS TO THINK ABOUT BEFORE THE NEXT STUDY

Have I ever done something for the Lord and a very short time later things just seemed to fall apart?

All that comes from Satan attacking you. He wants you back!

OT (Psalm 141:3-4) [3] Set a guard, O LORD, over my mouth; keep watch over the door of my lips! [4] Do not let my heart incline to any evil, to busy myself with wicked deed in company with men who work iniquity and let me not eat of their delicacies!

NT (1 Corinthians 10:13) No temptation has overtaken you that is not common to man. God is faithful, and he will not let you be tempted beyond your ability, but with the temptation he will also provide the way of escape, that you may be able to endure it.

Meat and Potatoes

(Do not give up on yourself.)

I know I have missed quite a few mornings with You, Lord. I apologize. Please help me stay grounded in You. I think I need that the most.

Yes, you do need that the most. That is why I will never give up on you, so please do not give up on yourself.

Mmm . . . I thought when I missed our time together, I was giving up on You, but I guess I am giving up on myself when I stop listening to you.

Yes. Listen to me, my people. I am not the one that needs guidance, help, hope and such; you are. I came to earth to save you, but I also came to give you abundant life. I did my part. When you stop seeking that abundant life-- let's say by turning down your switch—you are actually giving up on yourself because you are the ones that benefit from what I offer, not me. How do you think I feel when you do that?

You may answer that you think I am frustrated. No. When you turn your switch down you are the frustrated ones, I am the sad one. How do you think Father feels? Have you ever had children that went off on their own ways and did not communicate with you much? How did you feel? Did you have concern about them because you would not be able to help them if something bad happened? Well, that is how Father feels. That is how I feel.

I went through a lot to give you abundant life. Please do not throw that away! Please do not give up on yourselves? We love you and you are very precious to us. Please turn your switches back up!

Study 13 – Do God's Will (part 6)

The commands of Jesus teach you how to live as a child of God. Everything from how to treat God, how to represent Him, to worship Him, to follow Him, to how to treat each other and what to do if you are treated unfairly by one of your brothers or sisters in Christ. These commands cover how to treat others, from lowly people to rich, from children to enemies, from the sick and possessed and widows and families. It shows us what to do in all kinds of circumstances, and what to do if we mess up.

These are the things that Jesus did while on earth. These are the things that you should do while here on earth as His representative.

Now we will look at the Ten Commandments of God; first we will look at some history leading up to them.

Joseph was the second youngest child of Jacob. He was favored by His father, which made His older brothers jealous. They decided to get rid of him.

(Genesis 37:18-24) **A.** What was Reuben planning to do with Joseph later?

(Genesis 37:31-34) Reuben left them, and while he was gone the other brothers sold Joseph to a slave trader, and he was taken to Egypt as a slave. The brothers told their father that an animal killed Joseph. **B.** How were they able to convince their father of that?

Read about Joseph's time as a slave and how he became the Governor of all Egypt. (Genesis chapters 39-41)

During the famine that came upon the land, Jacob sent his sons to Egypt to buy wheat for the family. They did not know that Joseph was the Governor of Egypt because Joseph used an interpreter. They thought he was Egyptian because he dressed and talked like one. (Genesis chapters 42-44)

Eventually Joseph told his brothers who he really was and brings his family to Egypt where they excel. (Genesis 45-48)

Years later Joseph was on his deathbed and told his brothers that God was going to take the Israelites out of the foreign land and to the promised land.

(Genesis 50:24-26) **C.** What promise was Joseph's brothers and ancestors held accountable for when the Israelites left Egypt?

About 100 years after the death of Joseph, a new king arose in Egypt who did not know the history of the Israelites. All he saw was the possibility that there were so many of them that they could revolt and wipe him out, so he made them slaves.

(Exodus 1:8-14) **D.** What happened when the Israelites were oppressed more?

The Israelites were slaves for over 300 years when God had Moses bring them out of Egypt. Read Exodus chapters 2-4 if you want to learn more about Moses and how God chose him to lead the Israelites. Read Exodus chapters 5-12 if you want to learn how God sent the plagues to convince Pharaoh to let the people go.

After Moses brought the Israelites out of Egypt, they walked to Mount Sinai where God gave Moses the commandments. Moses was dealing with people who had never been free, and they did not know how to live as free people. God had to give the commandments that would show them how to live free. If He had not done so, there would have been chaos. The commandments gave them structure, purpose, and harmony just as they can do today.

PAGES (1st) 70-73   (2nd) 72-74

Read the commandments one at a time and read the comments and questions in this study, before moving to the next. Write down what each law is.

No. 1: (Exodus 20:1-2)

God reminds the people that He is the one who saved them. He knew that His people would be tempted to follow the gods of the nations that bordered the promised land, and he tells them not to do that.

(Isaiah 44:6-8) **1a** What does the LORD say about Himself in verse 6?

Other "gods" were demons masquerading as gods. There is no Rock among them, just rocks. The real Rock is Jesus. Since demons are from the spiritual realm they can do supernatural things, which makes people believe they are real gods, however, they are fake, or false gods because they cannot create. Only the real God can create. False gods can only corrupt what God has already created because they have no authority of their own.

The only authority the demons have is from people who have handed over their God given authority to Satan who rules the demons.

No. 2: (Exodus 20:4-6)

Often humans make images or idols of things that God has created: cows, pigs, sun, moon, goats, birds, or humans. This is **IDOLATRY: the worship of a physical object as a god.** (Encyclopedia

Britannica/Britannica, n.d.) It is putting the created before the Creator. Idolatry is a very serious thing!

(Isaiah 44:9–11) **2a** All the people that fashion and worship idols will be terrified and what else?

God was making a new covenant with His people. It was based on the laws that God gave Moses. If someone broke the laws, they sinned against God. The iniquity of that sin fell onto the descendants of that person to sometimes the fourth generation.

(Exodus 20:5) This verse mentions iniquity.

INIQUITY: immoral or grossly unfair behavior. (Merriam- Webster, 2024) Iniquity is not the sin; it is what happens inside a person after they sin. Sin is what happens when you violate, or disobey, the laws of God. Iniquity is the immoral behavior that occurs in someone's life after he sins, and this could carry on for generations because the iniquity (unholy behavior), was passed down from generation to generation. The children were taught that it was normal behavior, and it could take upwards of four generations to change their ways, to turn from that iniquity and repent.

God was not punishing the children for something the parent did, but He was allowing the wickedness (the behavior) of the wicked to follow the children until they repented and turned away from the iniquity, because He gave people free will. Unless they choose to repent, they will suffer the consequences of their actions, which can affect generations.

The verse says God is a jealous God. This word was translated from the root word "zelos" which is also the root word for "zealous." (Merriam-Webster, 2024) **Zealous** is more appropriate here, in that "zealous" has a positive connotation, **meaning passionate and eager.** God is very passionate about His people. When persons turn away from God, or put someone or something above Him, He is passionate and eager for those persons to repent and turn back to Him and put Him first in their lives.

The word **jealous** has a negative connotation, **meaning suspicious and resentful**. We apply this word to how humans may react to someone turning away from them or loving someone more than them. They react with anger and resentment and may respond negatively with belittling or violence. They react from emotions; God acts from righteousness. God will not respond negatively, but He will let people make their own decisions, and sometimes they suffer consequences caused by the decisions they have made.

God's goal is for people to repent of their Idolatry and make Him first in their lives. However, if they never do and then physically die, they are separated from God forever because they are spiritually dead.

(Romans 6:23) **2b** What is the gift of God spoken of in that verse?

In other words, Eternal Life belongs to those who have made Jesus the Lord of their lives by believing in how He thought, in what He said, in what He did and in how He treated people, believing God's Word (the Truth) and living out that truth. It is a lifestyle, not just religion. If you believe, then you will do likewise; It is either blessings from the Lord, and life, or curses from the world, and death. It is your choice.

No. 3: (Exodus 20:7)

3a What does it say about you if you disobey this law?

IN VAIN: without a result. (King James Bible Online, n.d.) You are to declare, pray, or do in the Lord's name. However, if you use His name inappropriately, or with insincerity, there will be no good results from that. You are giving Him a bad name and there could actually be negative results. If you claim to be Christian and say you are a child of God, but you act unholy, you have taken His name in vain. In other words, you say you are a Christian, taken His name, but you are living unholy. It is not just about saying His name inappropriately, but it is also living your life inappropriately, living your life in a way that is contrary to what you claim. In the world's eyes it is disgracing His name, giving Him a bad reputation.

No. 4: (Exodus 20:8-11)

The religious leaders added many laws to the ones that God had given them; there were more than 600. A person could not even pick up their bed on the Sabbath, because that was considered work. The religious leaders got nit-picky; they went to the extreme. When Jesus wanted to heal a man on the Sabbath, the Pharisees tried to trap Him. Jesus handled the situation with such wisdom.

(Matthew 12:9-13) **4a** When the Pharisees asked Jesus a question, how did He respond to that question? **4b** What did He say about a sheep and a man? So, if you are doing something good on the Sabbath, it is acceptable, if you do it to serve another, not for selfish reasons.

No. 5: (Exodus 20:12)

This is the first command connected with a promise. **5a** What is it?

No. 6: (Exodus 20:13)

This is often mistranslated as "kill." **6a** What is the difference between kill and murder? (See book)

No. 7: (Exodus 20:14)

Whatever is in your heart is taken very seriously by God and should be taken seriously by you. God wants you to guard your heart. **7a** What do you think that means?

(Proverbs 4:23) "Keep your heart with all vigilance, for from it flow the springs of life." Other translations say a wellspring of life. **WELLSPRING: a source of continuing supply.** ("Merriam-Webster, 2024) Whatever is in your heart will bubble up into your life. If you want to represent God in this world, then keep close watch over your heart, because it is very easy to be distracted by worldly desires.

No. 8: (Exodus 20:15)

8a Why do you think people steal? God says to trust Him to give you what you need. (Philippians 4:6) He will take care of you. (Ephesians 4:28) **8b** Why should the thief quit stealing and work instead?

No. 9: (Exodus 20:16)

To bear false witness is to lie. Liars have no place in heaven. (Revelation 21:8) **9a** What is portioned out to liars?

No. 10: (Exodus 20:17)

10a What does the verse say you are not to covet? **10b** Who is your neighbor? **10c** What do you imagine the world would be like if we all lived according to God's will?

11. What does John 14:23 say? These commandments given to us by Jesus and Father God are a litmus test of how much we love God.

LITMUS TEST: a test in which a single factor (such as an attitude, event, or fact) is decisive. (Merriam-Webster 2024)

DECISIVE: unmistakable, unquestionable. (Webster's Dictionary 1828-Online, n.d.)

These commandments from Jesus and Father God are vital to your spiritual health. It is also vital to the unity of Christ's Body.

THINGS TO THINK ABOUT BEFORE THE NEXT STUDY

What commandments have I ignored over the last year?

OT (Jeremiah 31:31-33) [31] "Behold, the days are coming, declares the LORD, when I will make a new covenant with the house of Israel and the house of Judah, [32] not like the covenant that I made with their fathers on the day when I took them by the hand to bring them out of the land of Egypt, my covenant that they broke, though I was their husband, declares the LORD. [33] For this is the covenant that I will make with the house of Israel after those days, declares the LORD: I will put my law within them, and I will write it on their hearts. And I will be their God, and they shall be my people.

NT (John 15:10) If you keep my commandments, you will abide in my love, just as I have kept my Father's commandments and abide in his love.

Meat and Potatoes

(Code of Conduct)

Our commandments are meant to be obeyed, not because we are tyrants, but because we love you. These commandments are to help you live the life we ordained for you and for my people to live in harmony with each other.

These commandments are principles that give you a solid foundation in my kingdom and my system of belief. I have set my people apart from the world, and these principles set you apart from the world's beliefs. You are to be a Holy people. These commandments help you to be holy. They are the principles that must be followed so people will know that you are my children.

Study 14 – Reach Out to Others

By following God's will, you are now equipped to fulfill your purpose. God wants you to bring more people into His Ekklesia, the Body of Christ. This is what Jesus called His "church." (More on that later.)

PAGES (1st) 74 – 78   (2nd) 75-79

1. What does God say about the people that reject Him?

2. How many people does God want saved in the worldwide revival that has begun?

3. What is inside you that makes it possible for you to do your purpose? (John 14:26) God's Glory is His presence in you as the Holy Spirit. **4.** According to the book, your purpose does what for you? People who live in darkness do not know the Good News. (2 Corinthians 4:3-5) **5.** What is Christ according to verse four?

6. According to the book what dissipates the darkness?

(John 9:5**) "As long as I am in the world, I am the light of the world."** Jesus is no longer here in the physical realm. You need to take that light into the world because you are His body now. He is in the world now through you. (Matthew 5:14-16**) 7.** Why must you let your light shine before others?

8. In the vision of the lighthouse, what did the dust balls represent?

9. Why were they able to be seen? **10.** According to Jesus' interpretation of the vision, what does the room represent?

11. Why couldn't the Holy Spirit send the light out into the world at first? **12.** What are the two lessons learned from this vision?

(2 Corinthians 13:5) **13.** What does the verse say you should realize about yourself? **14.** Are you operating in the faith? Determine if you are being led by Holy Spirit or by Satan's influence. In whatever you do, examine yourself to know who is influencing you in each situation, because the outcome will be determined by who is influencing you.

You need to declare God's truth out loud. People of the world cannot hear God's voice, so you voice His truth aloud so that it can manifest into the physical realm so the people of the world can hear it. Remember, God does not have a physical voice. You are His physical voice.

15. Why is it sometimes difficult for family members to believe that you are an active disciple of Jesus? **16.** What is the way to minister to your family? **17.** Besides being the example of Jesus, what is the best way to minister to people you associate with? **18.** What is an important thing to do with people you do not know?

19. What should you not do when you see homeless people? (Luke 4:18-19) You are to represent Jesus. He has anointed you to do what He was anointed to do.

In these situations, you are planting seeds. **20.** Who waters them? His job is to save people. **21.** What is your job?

The book says that meeting a personal need of someone is critical to that person's salvation. **22.** What might be a reason that meeting someone's felt need is critical?

A felt need is a physical need that persons consider one of the most important things missing in their lives. Meeting someone else's felt need is also very important to you as a disciple of Jesus. (Matthew 25:31-46) **23.** If you do not meet the felt needs of people when you can, what is a possible outcome for you?

24. When healing someone, what must you use to be able to do that? (Luke 10:19) This verse is referring to your authority over spiritual enemies. (Ephesians 6:12) **25.** Who do you wrestle against? When you take authority over the evil spirits that affect this world, you are then able to change the physical circumstances, because you have broken the stronghold they had over people. You have the power of the Holy Spirit to change things, sometimes through miracles.

Notice what Jesus said. (John 14:12-14) Notice that He did not say only His apostles would do these things, He said that those that believe in Him, His followers, would do them. That is you if you have made Jesus the Lord of your life.

Remember: Believe in Jesus; in what He thought, in what He said, in what He did, and in how He treated people. If you believe in Him, you will follow Him, which means you will pattern your life after His.

THINGS TO THINK ABOUT BEFORE THE NEXT STUDY

How can I let the light of Jesus shine brighter through me?

OT (Psalms 119:130) The unfolding of your words gives light; it imparts understanding to the simple.

NT (2 Corinthians 4:6) For God, who said, "Let light shine out of darkness," has shone in our hearts to give the light of the knowledge of the glory of God in the face of Jesus Christ.

Meat and Potatoes

(Light Dissipates Darkness)

I bless all my people that spread my message in words, voice, and in action. This is so very important, especially in these dark times on earth. I AM light and I am in You, so wherever you go, you are taking my light there. You see with my light which dissipates the darkness. What does that word mean? **DISSIPATE: Disappear or cause to disappear.** (Definitions C Meanings of Words/Britannica Dictionary, n.d.)

People think darkness is tangible, but it isn't. **TANGIBLE: Real and not imaginary; able to be shown, touched, or experienced by the physical senses.** (Merriam-Webster, 2024)

I did not create darkness; it is just absence of light. When light comes, there is no darkness. I am talking about darkness in the spiritual realm, as well. Hence, wherever you, my people are, there should be no darkness around you in the spiritual realm, because you carry my light with you. However, too many times, others are still in darkness when they see my people, because their power switches are turned down, or even off. Darkness dissipates IF my people allow their lights to shine.

Many of my people focus on the darkness in this world and cannot see my Truth and become afraid and discouraged. They are looking at the spiritual darkness with their carnal eyes, which shuts off my light in them. As a result, they have limited Holy Spirit, and He is the one that brings my power and light to you. It is that spiritual connection that allows my power and light to flow through you into the darkness. People are not afraid of the dark; they are afraid of what is in the darkness. My light allows you to see what the darkness is hiding. It exposes the lies and deceit.

Unfortunately, the intangible darkness has made it possible for the tangible to occur in the darkness; all things that Satan wants to hide from people. Darkness allows those things to continue, because people cannot see the evil that is the cause of what is happening in the world. You must take my light into the darkness of the world, my people, or the evil will continue to grow through Satan's deception.

Now is the time Church, to turn your switches back on so that my light can shine and expose the enemy's schemes and the evil that is behind all that is happening. Take my light into the world so that others can see the Truth. The sooner you get your switches turned back up, the sooner this evil can be eradicated. Expose the lies by letting the Truth shine brightly.

I love you!

Study 15 – Why We Need to Reach Out

Now that you know you need to reach out to others, study some of the reasons why you need to reach out.

PAGES (1st) 78–84   (2nd) 80-85

1. What are the four reasons why you need to reach out?

Remember that giving your life to God means doing God's will as well.

(James 2:17) **2.** What does the verse say is dead if it has no works? It is not enough to believe that God is, Satan believes that. (James 2:19) You must believe what He says in His Word, then live it out.

If you believe God, then you will do His will, which is the part that shows others the love that God has for them. They will not be saved if they do not see any reason to be saved. (James 2:14-16) The verse asks, "What good is it to tell someone to go in peace if you have not met their felt needs?" **3.** Answer that question.

4. According to the book, what does God want for every person?

5. What are they to Him? **6.** What is the reason God can only exercise His authority on earth through humans? **7.** How can His authority manifest in the world? **MANIFEST: to show something clearly, through signs or actions.** That takes faith.

(1 John 5:4) **8.** What is the victory that has overcome the world? God says in the book that most of the world thinks He has no authority. **9.** Why is that? **10.** What is the result of that?

The people of the world think they have their own authority to solve their own problems. **11.** Who is really calling the shots? He does that through his deception. (Revelation 12:7-12) **12.** Who is Satan the deceiver of?

The book says that some people believe they only answer to themselves, not to anyone else. **13.** What does God say about that?

14. Why do they not know that Satan is in control of the world?

Another reason people do not know Satan is in control of the world is found in (2 Corinthians 4:3-4) They cannot see the light of the Gospel. **15.** Why?

In the book God did not say to just "tell" the people the truth.

16. What did He say you are to do with His truth? **17.** What does that mean?

(Psalm 86:11) **18.** Why did David want the LORD to teach him His way? The fear mentioned in this case means to have reverential awe. You must honor Him and His name, for it is the name above all names. Walking in truth is to think like Jesus would, say what Jesus would say, do what Jesus would do and treat people how Jesus would treat them.

The book says that people search their whole lives to find a worldly thing that will fill a void inside them. It seems like they are never satisfied no matter how much "stuff" or money they get, it is never enough. Some of the unhappiest people are those with the most wealth and money. **19.** What is the only thing of God that can fill that void? **20.** What makes wholeness possible in a person?

21. What does the book say would happen if Jesus had not made His tremendous sacrifice for humans?

22. Why couldn't Jesus be born of a human mother that had been impregnated by a human father?

23. When did Jesus overcome death?

24. When are humans no longer bound by the restraints of the physical realm?

25. What was an old, repurposed cupboard that was made into a coffee bar, compared to in the book?

26. What does God do with broken and dirty people?

27. Who is important to God?

28. What is the message God wants you to carry into the world?

God wants all people to abide with Him so they can experience abundant life and harmony with each other. That would be a win/win situation for all.

THINGS TO THINK ABOUT BEFORE THE NEXT STUDY

When have I ever used my God given authority on God's behalf? OT (Genesis 1:26) Then God said, "Let us make man in our image,

after our likeness. And let them have dominion over the fish of the sea and over the birds of the heavens and over the livestock and over all the earth and over every creeping thing that creeps on the earth."

NT (Luke 10:19) Behold, I have given you authority to tread on serpents and scorpions, and over all the power of the enemy, and nothing shall hurt you.

Meat and Potatoes

(Fill the void with Jesus)

I was drinking coffee and commented to the Lord that I wish coffee tasted as good as it smelled. He responded as follows:

Many things in the world are like that. They look, smell and sound like really awesome things, but when you experience them, they are okay, but not at all what you anticipated.

I want to teach everyone the Truth, but unfortunately not everyone has a relationship with me. Many know who I am, but they do not know me. This applies to some of my own people that have their switches turned down.

I also want to teach the people who are not saved, but they must accept me as Savior and Lord. I want to save them, but to do that they need to make me the Lord of their lives. (Smiling) This is where those good looking, smelling, and sounding things come into play. People think that those things are most important because they seem so appealing, and will satisfy their desires, their yearnings. However, when they acquire and experience those things, it is a less than expected experience. What people think will be awesome turns out to be less than satisfying.

However, when they experience me, everything else becomes less important, which means those things can be more satisfying, because people's expectations of them are lower; more realistic. Do you understand what I am saying?

I think so. When people don't know you, they look to physical things to fulfill a yearning in them. Their expectations are too high; higher than what those things can actually deliver. They are counting on those things to fill a void in them that only you can fill, therefore, once acquired, they are less than satisfying. Once they know You, that void is filled with your presence, so now they can enjoy other things without the unrealistic expectations, because the yearning they had for what You have to offer has been satisfied.

Yes. The yearning people have is for the things that only I can fulfill because they are actually yearning for the spiritual things that I give. People are spiritual beings, and they yearn for spiritual things that they need. That void cannot be satisfied with worldly things. Without me, people's expectations are too high for the things of the world, thereby, not satisfying when received. This is why most people who have acquired many physical things never seem to have enough, they are never satisfied.

Choose me, people. You will be satisfied.

Study 16 – Why the Church Has Become So Broken

Because of Satan's influence in this world, the "Church" has become broken. It needs to be restored.

PAGES (1st) 85 – 92   (2nd) 86-94

1. What has happened because of God's people not doing what they were created to do and not being who they were created to be?

2. What was the main difference between Jesus and His disciples?

3. Why could Holy Spirit live in Jesus?

4. What is the difference between living *for* the presence of God and living *from* His presence? You might also live for the presence if you have your switch turned off and He cannot influence you.

5. When were the disciples able to live from the presence? (Acts 2:2-9) **6.** When the Holy Spirit came into the room, what did it sound like? **7.** What did it look like?

It is the same for you now, as it was for the disciples then. You should be living from the Spirit, not for the Spirit, because, if you have made Jesus the lord of your life, Holy Spirit already lives in you.

8. What is the problem with something that is broken? **9.** In the book, what are the four reasons why the Church has become so broken?

10. What does infiltrate mean?

One definition says to become part of a group in order to get information or to influence the way that group thinks or behaves.

This is what Satan has done. He is the one that influences behavior in the worldly realm.

11. How long has Satan tried to destroy the Church? **12.** Twice he tried to do this by influencing people to do what?

(Exodus 1:15-22) **13.** Who thwarted his plans the first time? **14.** When Pharaoh asked why the midwives let the male children live, what was their answer?

(Matthew 2:13-15) **15.** Who thwarted Satan's plans the second time? **16.** How did he thwart Satan's plan? **17.** When Jesus died on the cross, what did Satan not realize?

(Acts 7:54-60) **18.** What happened to Stephen? It says in Acts 8 that one of most ardent supporters of the persecution of the Church became one of God's most important advocates. (Acts 8:1-3) He approved Stephen's execution. **19.** Who was he?

Later, when he was saved, he became an apostle of God. He taught in the local synagogue. However, when God sent him and Barnabas out into the world, God's Word refers to him as Paul. This is where some leaders of the modern Church determined that God renamed him Paul, which is what I was taught. However, God told me recently that He did not rename him Paul but referred to him in scripture, after Acts 12, by the Roman translation of his name. Prior to that he was known in scripture by his Hebrew name of Saul because most people whom he talked to were Jews. Paul was a Jew, but he was also an actual citizen of Rome. Since he now was going out into the world where most people were not Jewish, God switched from using Saul to using Paul in His Word.

He did this because most of the people He spoke to could relate more to that name than his Hebrew name.

20. According to the book, what was the outcome of the infiltration of the Church? No wonder the world is so dark.

21. When can you make a difference in someone else's life? When you live from your carnal mind and let the physical realm dominate you, you are not putting your trust in the Lord and living from the Spirit. You have your switch turned down. That means you are not letting the light of Jesus shine through you.

COLLUDING: cooperating in a secret or unlawful way in order to deceive or gain an advantage over others. (Merriam-Webster, 2024)

22. Why are certain leaders in the Church intentionally opposing God and His divine plan? **23.** What will happen to the people that offend, hurt, or kill children?

(1 Timothy 6:3-5) **24.** What do depraved people who have not heard God's truth, imagine that godliness is? They have a false godliness because they think they will have fame, power, or prestige.

25. How are God's people enabling Satan? (James 1:22-27) **26.** What does verse 22 tell you to do? **27.** What must God's people do to show His love to others? It should be your lifestyle. You live out God's truth, ministering to people outside of the church walls.

28. What are the five reasons the book gives for God's people not doing what they are supposed to do? **29.** What does God say His Church must start doing? He also tells His Church to stop doing something. **30.** What is it?

31. What is God counting on you to do?

You must be an active Christian, or you are not really a Christian. We all fail to do God's will at some point, however, that is where repenting comes into play. Remember, repent means to actually turn from the disobedience and ask for forgiveness. Here is what God told me once:

I need mature people in my army, not babies or children in their faith. So, keep pressing in, keep studying my Word, and keep following me and doing my will. Always keep relying on Holy Spirit to guide you, to teach you, and to show you the way. He is the one that helps you to understand my Truth and gives you the wisdom and power to do my will. Keep your switch turned up high!

THINGS TO THINK ABOUT BEFORE THE NEXT STUDY

When have I enabled Satan by not doing something that I should have done, or by not saying something I should have said?

OT (2 Samuel 23:2) The Spirit of the LORD speaks by me; his word is on my tongue.

NT (1 John 5:1-12) [1] Everyone who believes that Jesus is the Christ has been born of God, and everyone who loves the Father loves whoever has been born of him. [2] By this we know that we love the children of God when we love God and obey his commandments.

[3] For this is the love of God, that we keep his commandments. And his commandments are not burdensome. [4] For everyone who has been born of God overcomes the world. And this is the victory that has overcome the world—our faith. [5] Who is it that overcomes the world except the one who believes that Jesus is the Son of God?

Meat and Potatoes

(The twerp)

I was confused about my feelings. I told Jesus that He was my best friend. He knew that I was questioning something in my mind, so He asked me what I was thinking.

Well. . . I almost feel like I'm . . . ah . . . disappointing Holy Spirit when I say You are my best friend, because He is a best friend, too. It's . . . ah . . .confusing.

You need not be confused. Holy Spirit and I are one with Father. When you say something to one of us, you are saying it to all three of us, so we do not get offended. You are a treasure to us.

Whew, good. (A thought entered my mind) Ooo . . . Satan is a pain in the neck. I was going to respond to the treasure comment by saying, "Oh, fool's gold?" But then I realized that it was Satan putting that disparaging thought into my mind, trying to belittle me. The little . . . um . . .

Twerp?

(Chuckling) Well, I didn't know whether I should say it or not.

*Well, what is the meaning of **TWERP?***

I'll look it up . . . **A silly, insignificant, or contemptible person.**

(Merriam-Webster n.d.)

That pretty much applies. He is silly to think that he can win when he has already lost. He is insignificant in the fact that he has no power of his own, or influence, unless people let him influence them.

He is contemptible because he disregards us and what is right, plus, he thinks my people are worthless and deserving of scorn. He thinks of himself too highly; he is narcissistic and has an excessive interest in himself. But he is lowly, even though he thinks he is high because people give him power. But it is a false sense of power, which he will realize when he is thrown into hell for eternity.

His main target is you, my people, so do not give him the power! You have authority over him, because greater AM I in you, than he in the world. Rebuke him, decree against him, and declare my Truth. He has no response to it because he has no defense against the Truth, my Word.

Remember, my Word, my Truth is a double-edged sword that you can defend yourself with, but you can also strike with it, and Satan must back off.

I AM! He is not. He's a twerp.

Study 17 – How to Restore the Church (Part 1)

The only hope for the people of the world is the vibrant, bold, fearless Church, with the heart of Jesus.

PAGES (1st) 93 –101   (2nd) 94-102

Name the two steps in this section that you must do to become a part of the vibrant, fearless Church.

The church today is quite different from what Jesus originally set up. **2.** Why is that?

3. What was Satan's reason for infiltrating the Church? **4.** Why?

The group Jesus created was not a religious organization, but a secular one, an ekklesia. The primary place of ministering for the Ekklesia, was in the marketplace, not in a church building. They went where the need was, they did not require the needy to come to a church building to be ministered to.

PENTECOST: the seventh Sunday after Easter observed as a Christian church festival in memory of the appearance of the Holy Spirit to the apostles. (Merriam-Webster, n.d.)

(Acts 2:1-41) **5.** According to the book, what did the Ekklesia do after Pentecost? **6.** What was the result of that?

7. How was the Ekklesia able to spread the Word to over a million people in a thirty thousand square mile area, in three years, with no modern transportation or technological advances?

As more people joined, they did the same. Call it the ripple effect. The book says that the Ekklesia members ministered 24/7. **8.** How was that possible? They were full-time ministers of God's kingdom. It was a lifestyle.

In the original language, Ekklesia or assembly was used 115 times in the New Testament. It is translated as church in all but three of those times. Look at the original language of Matthew 16:18 [From Strong's Concordance.] We will use the King James Version. In the concordance the number for the word "church" is 1577. When we look up that number in the concordance, the original word was Ekklhsia, pronounced as ek-klay-see'-ah. It says in the book that ekklesia means a calling out of citizens from their homes to a public place to conduct governmental business.

For the Romans, their ekklesia was the senate. Jesus's Ekklesia conducts governmental business for the kingdom of God. We are ambassadors of heaven. Just as the senate was a ruling counsel for Rome's kingdom, Jesus's Ekklesia is a ruling counsel for God's kingdom.

Remember what God originally told Adam and Eve. (Genesis 1:28) God gave humans His authority to have dominion on the earth. Their goal was to extend God's kingdom throughout the world. **DOMINION: the right to govern or rule or determine.** (Merriam-Webster, 2024) **AUTHORITY: power for a specific purpose with specified limits.** (Merriam-Webster, 2024) **POWER: possession of ability to wield force, authority, or influence.** (Merriam Webster, 2024)

You are a part of God's ruling counsel here on earth if Jesus is your Lord, you are a child of God, and you are doing God's will. This was how it was in the Garden of Eden before Adam and Eve sinned.

According to the book:

9. What did the Ekklesia do that allowed people to see that God truly loved them, cared about them, and wanted them to be a part of His family?

What does the word "church" relate to? The messages and activities within the church are primarily centered around the members, not the populace. **11.** Is that what Jesus told His disciples to do?

12. Why did King James tell his scribes to change the word assembly (meaning the Ekklesia) to the word church? He felt that it was his right as a king to have complete control over everything.

Today, the churches are split between social churches and conservative churches. Unless we unite as one people, Christ's Body, under one Head, the whole work of God cannot be done. This is the major problem with religion: God's people are broken up into multiple bodies, with separate heads. In the Ekklesia of Jesus there is one body and one head and everyone is equal. There is no distinction between people's backgrounds, gender, religion, social status, race, wealth, or anything else in the worldly realm.

The Ekklesia is a spiritual organization and must be guided by the Holy Spirit. Everything we do and say should be centered on God's principles and Truth, and we should live it out because it is supposed to be a 24/7 lifestyle, not a religion. Going to church is very important to many people, but when they leave the four walls of the church, they must live out the truth and pass God's love on to others; sadly, most do not. They are still living from their physical senses and not from the spiritual senses, meaning they are still babies in their faith.

13. What are the four dimensions of poverty? All four dimensions must be addressed to abolish poverty. **14.** Why will governmental programs never abolish poverty?

The Ekklesia addresses all four. **15.** How do they address the motivational dimension? **16.** How do they address the relational dimension? **17.** How do they address the material dimension? **18.** How do they address the spiritual dimension?

Watch the series *The Chosen* to get a sense of how the Ekklesia operated.

I do not believe that most of God's people truly understand what Jesus did for us. The book references Revelation 5:1-3. John was the apostle that wrote Revelation. He was taken in a vision to heaven and told to write down what he saw. He saw when heaven was looking for a person to be the sacrifice for all humanity, but no one was worthy. John knew how lost people were and how dark the world had become.

(Revelation 5:4-5) John sobbed when the angel said no one was worthy to open the scroll. Then he was shown Jesus as the sacrificial lamb, which meant that Jesus was worthy to overcome the darkness and death. (Revelation 5:6-14) John was in eternity in his vision, and he saw back into eternity when heaven was looking for someone to be the redeemer. Jesus had not yet become the Redeemer, but when John saw Jesus volunteer, he saw Him as the already sacrificed lamb, because in John's timeframe Jesus had already been crucified, died, and rose again. John saw the past, the present, and the future all at the same time. This is how eternity is. There is no timeframe in the spiritual realm, eternity, and you are not bound by time because time does not exist there.

19. The book says that Jesus agonized about the torture He was going to have to bear, but what else did He agonize over?

Take a few minutes to think about how devastating that would have been. For the first time ever, Jesus was going to be separated from Father God. When that happened Jesus felt abandoned and forsaken. Now remember, His disciples had already abandoned Him, and now since He lost His connection with Father God, He felt forsaken. Of course, Father God had not forsaken Him, but because there was no connection there, Jesus felt abandoned. When Jesus says, "My God, my God, why have you forsaken me?" it was the only time that Jesus did not refer to God has His father. He lost His personal connection with Father God because Holy Spirit was no longer with Him.

This is what happens when a person is going through trials and tribulations without a personal connection to God, or they have turned their switch down. They feel abandoned and forsaken, but be assured, God has not forsaken them!

20. If your sins have been forgiven, then why don't you automatically spend eternity with God? **21.** Why are you worthy to pass on God's message to other people? DO NOT EVER FORGET THAT!

THINGS TO THINK ABOUT BEFORE THE NEXT STUDY

There was a ripple effect when the Ekklesia ministered to people. Using a calculator, figure out how long it would take to reach everyone on earth if you spoke to seven people and the next day, you and they would speak to seven people who then would speak to seven people the next day, and so on. Each day every person, including you, would speak to seven more people.

OT (Isaiah 61:10-11) [10] I will greatly rejoice in the LORD; my soul shall exult in my God, for he has clothed me with the garments of salvation; he has covered me with the robe of righteousness, as a bridegroom decks himself like a priest with a beautiful headdress, and as a bride adorns herself with her jewels. [11] For as the earth brings forth its sprouts, and as a garden because what is sown in it to sprout up, so the Lord GOD will cause righteousness and praise to sprout up before all the nations.

NT (2 Corinthians 4:13-18) [13] Since we have the same spirit of faith according to what has been written, "I believed, and so I spoke," we also believe, and so we also speak, [14] knowing that he who raised the Lord Jesus will raise us also with Jesus and bring us with you into his presence. [15] For it is all for your sake, so that as grace extends to more and more people it may increase thanksgiving, to the glory of God. [16] So we do not lose heart. Though our outer self is wasting away, our inner self is being renewed day by day. [17] For this light momentary affliction is preparing for us an eternal weight of glory beyond all comparison,

[18] as we look not to the things that are seen but to the things that are unseen. For the things that are seen are transient, but the things that are unseen are eternal.

Meat and Potatoes

(Falling Away) A conversation with Holy Spirit

I AM always teaching. Any time we converse, I am teaching. When you read something, I am teaching. When you look at creation, I am teaching. When you sleep, I am teaching. No matter what you do or say, I am teaching. That little voice in your mind is me teaching. I am your conscience as a guide to the right or wrongness of your behavior. When you are acting unholy, I am still here teaching you. Many members of Jesus's body think that I leave them when they mess up, but that is not true. It was true when the old covenant was in force, because my presence would destroy sin which would have destroyed the person, but now we have a new covenant of Grace, because Yeshua paid the price for sin.

When a person sins, I am there to convict them of that sin, so they can repent and turn away from that unholiness.

Sometimes we, God's people, swat you away.

(Chuckling) You can try but you cannot swat me away because I am inside you. All you can do is stop listening to what I am saying. I am still here; you just choose to ignore me; it is a conscience decision you have made; a conscience decision to not do Father God's will.

Religion has taught "once saved, always saved," but saying a prayer does not determine if you have eternal life, it is based on doing Father's will or not doing it. When people choose to not do Father's will, they have chosen to do Satan's will, which means he is lord of their lives at that point, instead of Jesus. They have rejected Jesus, which means they have rejected Father, they have lost their reverential respect for Him. They are rejecting eternity with Him and will spend eternity without Him if they do not repent. Jesus suffered greatly for your salvation. That is why Father has given each person a chance to repent. Unfortunately, in these last days, many of our people will fall away because they have allowed themselves to be distracted by Satan's lies and stopped listening to me. (Hebrews 3:12-1S references that.)

The more you use your physical mind, the further away you get from God. The further away from God you get, the longer it takes to repent. The longer you take to repent, the more you begin to doubt God. The more you doubt God, the less of God's image you convey. The less of God's image you convey, the more you look like the people of the world. The more you look like the people of the world, the more you act like them. The more you act like them, the less faith you have in God. The less faith you have in God, the more you believe Satan's lies. The more you believe Satan's lies, the more you make Satan the lord of your life. The more you make Satan the lord of your life, the more fear creeps into your heart. The more fear that creeps into your heart, the less you do Father's will. The less you do Father's will, the greater the chance you have of spending eternity without Him. Is that what you want?

Study 18 – How to Restore the Church (part 2)

We have been studying about how God's people must be bold and fearless. In this study you will learn about six more things that will help you achieve boldness and fearlessly represent Jesus.

PAGES (1st) 101-115   (2nd) 102-115

One at a time write down the first two steps that is needed to restore the Church.

1. What is the first step?

Your essence, your being exists in the spiritual realm. Your body exists in the physical, worldly realm.

1a How were Adam and Eve disconnected from God when they sinned? **1b** Why was that necessary? **1c.** Why did their carnal minds have to take over to help them exist on the earth? When Jesus became the atonement for humankind's sin, He made it possible for humans to connect back up with Holy Spirit again and experience eternity once more. **1d** What brings eternity into the worldly realm?

1e Why will Satan do anything he can to keep you from understanding who you are in Christ? **1f** God wants humans to enjoy His creation, so what did He do to make it possible for your spirit to interact in the natural realm? **1g** Who is in control of the worldly realm? **1h** Why can't God Himself control what Satan does in the world?

1i So how can God's will manifest on earth? He must rely on people, you, to do His will on earth. **1j** The question is: CAN He rely on you? **1k** Why are most of God's people not using the authority Jesus redeemed for us?

If God was in control of the world, it would look a lot different than it does now! It would be like . . . well, the Garden of Eden. That was His divine will being done on earth as it is in heaven: perfection and harmony. There was harmony between God and humans, between humans and animals and between man and woman.

1L How does Satan control what goes on in this worldly realm? **1n.** What happens when you have no discernment from Holy Spirit? **1n** Why do Satan's lies manifest into your life?

You must declare God's truth, not voice Satan's lies. **DECLARE: to make known formally, officially, or explicitly.** (Definitions C Meanings of Words / Britannica Dictionary, n.d.) Remember: you are an ambassador of heaven. You are an official of God's ruling counsel here on earth and you are to officially declare God's truth as part of His Ekklesia. **1o** Do you?

Satan's battleground is your mind, which is why you must take your thoughts captive and throw them out; do not ignore them. They will fester in the back of your mind until they explode. Take authority over them and then throw them out. Get rid of them.

(2 Corinthians 10:3-5) **1p** What does the last half of verse 5 say? Remember: you do not have to sin if Jesus is Lord of your life. (James 4:7) "Submit yourselves therefore to God. Resist the devil, and he will flee from you." This is what Jesus did in the wilderness. (Matthew 4:10) Jesus took His thoughts captive and voiced scripture, the Truth. Satan tried three times to get Jesus to focus on his half-truths. Each time Jesus declared the Truth, so Satan left.

1q What is Satan's character defined by?

2. What is the second step?

Sometimes the hardest thing to do is to look at yourself with an open mind. Before you can turn from worldly ways, you must admit you are acting worldly, then repent. **2a** What is the outcome when you reason with your spiritual mind, looking at things with the "big picture" frame of mind?

In the conversation about fear, it says that emotion is derived from one's circumstances, mood, or relationship with others. It is based on the physical, worldly things and not on fact or truth. It is separate from reasoning or knowledge. When you are living worldly you live from your emotions. **2b** What happens that causes you to make bad decisions at that point? **2c** What is the problem with believing your feelings are the truth?

Truth is fact and does not change based on feelings. Notice that the book says truth is the quality or state of being true and that it is in accordance with fact or reality. Truth is based on those two things.

Emotions are based on what a person perceives to be truth at that time, which is Satan's deception through the mind. It is belief in His lies, not God's Truth, which is the real reality, not Satan's false reality. Notice that the false reality is always based on carnal things, not on spiritual things.

(Romans 8:6) "For to set the mind on the flesh is death, but to set the mind on the Spirit is life and peace." **2d** To set the mind on the flesh is what? **2e** To set the mind on the Spirit is what?

(Romans 12:2) **2f** The verse says you are not to be conformed to this world, but to be what? You cannot conform to this world and expect to do God's will. How many times has your life gone into a downward spiral because you were thinking with your carnal mind and making choices based on emotions instead of reasoning with your spirit? **2g** Name one. **2h** Why do you sometimes make bad decisions that cause negative things to happen?

2i According to the book, why do people think God hates them? **2j** Why can't people see that God's love is unconditional? This is why someone who is afraid of God must see His unconditional love applied to them before they can trust Him before they can see God's truth. God is asking His people, you, why they are not showing the deceived, fearful people His unconditional love. **2k** Do you need to respond to that question? Think about how many people are lost forever because we are not acting like the people we say we are.

We must act as God's Ekklesia and address spiritual matters through our physical actions. **2L** What are the four things that you must do?

THINGS TO THINK ABOUT BEFORE THE NEXT STUDY

Think about the differences and likenesses between our modern churches and the Ekklesia; physical and spiritual.

OT (Jeremiah 17:5–8) [5] Thus says the LORD: "Cursed is the man who trusts in man and makes flesh his strength, whose heart turns away from the LORD. [6] He is like a shrub in the desert and shall not see any good come. He shall dwell in the parched places of the wilderness, in an uninhabited salt land. [7] "Blessed is the man who trusts in the LORD, whose trust is the LORD. [8] He is like a tree planted by water, which sends out its roots by the stream, and does not fear when heat comes, for its leaves remain green, and is not anxious in the year of drought, for it does not cease to bear fruit."

NT (Hebrews 10:19–39) [19] Therefore, brothers, since we have confidence to enter the holy places by the blood of Jesus, [20] by the new and living way that he opened for us through the curtain, that is, through his flesh, [21] and since we have a great priest over the house of God, [22] let us draw near with a true heart in full assurance of faith, with our hearts sprinkled clean from an evil conscience and our bodies washed with pure water. [23] Let us hold fast the confession of our hope without wavering, for he who promised is faithful. [24] And let us consider how to stir up one another to love and good works, [25] not neglecting to meet together, as is the habit of some, but encouraging one another, and all the more as you see the Day drawing near. [26] For if we go on sinning deliberately after receiving the knowledge of the truth, there no longer remains a sacrifice for sins, [27] but a fearful expectation of judgment, and a fury of fire that will consume the adversaries. [28] Anyone who has set aside the law of Moses dies without mercy on the evidence of two or three witnesses. [29] How much worse punishment, do you think, will be deserved by the one who has trampled underfoot the Son of God, and has profaned the blood of the covenant by which he was sanctified, and has outraged the Spirit of grace? [30] For we know him who said, "Vengeance is mine; I will repay." And again, "The Lord will judge his people." [31] It is a fearful thing to fall into the hands of the living God.

Meat and Potatoes

(A talk with Jesus)

I told Jesus that I might need a mentor to help me gain confidence. This was His reply:

I can give you a mentor, but if you do not study my Word more a mentor will not help. You must know my Word because it is the Truth. A mentor shows you how to live out the truth, but if you do not know the truth you cannot live it out.

Well, that is simple enough.

Yes, it always has been, but humans have to complicate things. There is a difference between doing and living the truth. Doing is because you know the right thing to do, but living it is because it is a part of who you are now. It is a way of life for you.

So the truth must become a part of who I am . . . like how love is who you are.

Yes, it is my nature, it cannot be separated from me.

So truth must be my nature and should not be separated from me?

Not "should not" be separated but "cannot" be separated from you, like my disciples. When the disciples were "doing" they ran away when things got tough. Some even denied me. But afterwards, when they received Holy Spirit's power, Truth became a lifestyle for them, a part of their nature. What is the proof of that?

They died for it.

Yes. It was not just doctrine to them, but a way of life, a part of their nature. This is why you must study my Truth until it becomes your lifestyle. What is Romans 10:17?

Faith comes by hearing, and hearing by the Word of God.

Faith does not come by what others are doing, but by hearing my Word spoken by them, or better yet, hearing my Word spoken by you as you read my Word out loud. Make studying my Word a daily habit then live it out. The more you do that the more it becomes a part of who you are and the more you will live it out.

Wow.

Yep, simple.

Study 19 – How to Restore the Church (part 3)

One of the most important things you must do is to be conscience of what is influencing you as you live your life. Determine if you are being influenced by the world or by Holy Spirit.

(1st) 115-131   (2nd) 115-132

3. What is the next step to take to restore the Church?

To be who you were created to be, and do what you were ordained to do, you need a personal relationship with God. Remember, He is your spiritual Father. He cannot father you if you do not have a relationship with Him. It is truly the most important thing in your life! That is where you get the power and the wisdom to discern the truth.

3a Are you walking in the light of God in a strong relationship, or are you walking in the darkness of the world? (1 John 1:6) **3b** What does this verse say you do when you claim to have fellowship with God while you walk in darkness? (1 John 2:6) "Whoever says he abides in Him ought to walk in the same way He walked." (John 12:44-46) **3c** What does Jesus say in verse 46?

Remember, Jesus said that if you are truly His disciple you will know the truth and it will set you free. To know the truth you must have a relationship with God through His Holy Spirit, because He is the one that teaches you the truth. (John 16:13)" When the Spirit of truth comes, He will guide you into all the truth . . ."

Remember something else: When you are doing your own thing and it does not line up with God's will, than you are disparaging Jesus' name. You are giving Him a bad reputation, you Christian.

4. What is the next step to take?

4a Why does God want you never to be afraid to ask Him for help? (John 10:10) Jesus wants you to have abundant life. He does not want you to just exist or just to cope, He wants you to excel in abundance. **4b** What does the thief come to do? **4c** If Satan knows he has lost, why does he still try to get us to believe his lies?

5. What is the next step?

5a What are the five reasons that you must study God's Word and teachings?

It is crucial that you study God's Word, for that is His Truth. You are to live that Truth. To live it you must know it. (John 8:31-32) "So Jesus said to the Jews who had believed Him, "If you abide in my word, you are truly my disciples, and the truth will set you free."" Most translations of the Bible use either the word *abide* or *continue.* Both of the words come from the Greek word μένω (pronounced me'no) which is a verb meaning **to remain, to abide, to stay, to continue, to dwell, to endure**. How do you this? By focusing on the Word, living it out, making it a part of your daily life. In other words, it becomes a way of life.

5b In the verse above, what did Jesus say would happen if you abided in His word? **5c** What do you suppose you are set free from? That relationship with God, through Holy Spirit, is what allows you to discern, to recognize, the difference between Satan's deceitful lies and God's truth. In other words, you will be able to know what and where the lies are in your mind and around you.

God says that you must read what His prophets have written, but also to seek Him (a relationship with Him). **5d** Why must you seek God and desire time with Him? **5e** Why should you put your faith in Father God, Jesus, and Holy Spirit?

5f What does 2 Corinthians 5:7 say? **5g** Why does God need your help? **5h** Do you have confidence in your relationship with God? Faith and confidence are what you need to step out and do His will.

6. What is the next step?

6a God has no control over what happens in the worldly realm unless you do what? The book says to never forget your authority over Satan's evil plans. **6b** What are the encouraging words mentioned in 1 John 4:4? **6c** When you do not stand up to evil, what are you doing? This is why the world is in such terrible straits.

THINGS TO THINK ABOUT BEFORE THE NEXT STUDY

Think about what is going on in the world right now. How much of it happens because people do not have a personal relationship with God?Make a list.

OT (Isaiah 26:1-9) [1] In that day this song will be sung in the land of Judah: "We have a strong city; he sets up salvation as walls and bulwarks. [2] Open the gates, that the righteous nation that keeps faith may enter in. [3] You keep him in perfect peace whose mind is stayed on you, because he trusts in you. [4] Trust in the LORD forever, for the LORD GOD is an everlasting rock. [5] For he has humbled the inhabitants of the height, the lofty city. He lays it low, lays it low to the ground, casts it to the dust. [6] The foot tramples it, the feet of the poor, the steps of the needy." [7] The path of the righteous is level; you make level the way of the righteous. [8] In the path of your judgments, O LORD, we wait for you; your name and remembrance are the desire of our soul. [9] My soul yearns for you in the night; my spirit within me earnestly seeks you. For when your judgments are in the earth the inhabitants of the world learn righteousness.

NT (John 14:1) Let not your hearts be troubled. Believe in God; believe also in me.

Meat and Potatoes

(Seek the Truth) A conversation with Jesus

Each person must search out the Truth, for it is not being taught in most churches.

Who do You blame for that?

That is a loaded question, which does not have a single answer. Satan infiltrated the Church, so it all begins with him. However, it falls on the shoulders of my people, they have not searched out the Truth, they have just trusted what they have been told. Ultimately, it all comes down to the fact that every person makes a choice for themselves, so part of the blame rests on each one. But blame is not what I do, I took care of that on the cross, however I do hold people accountable for their actions, for the choices they make. That is their prerogative, a right Father has given them, free will.

My hope is that all my people will search out the Truth because that is what will set them free. If they are not free, they cannot help me set others free. You all have the keys of the kingdom, but unless you use them, you cannot be free or set anyone else free. I need my people to be free. My Ekklesia must teach people the Truth, for I am counting on them, the Remnant. The Truth is my love, not condemnation. People MUST see my love in action, not just to hear words. My Ekklesia LIVES the Truth, a lifestyle of ministering, of showing others my love.

Study 20 – How to Restore the Church (part 4)

We have been studying about how we need to be the light of Jesus.

Pages (1st) 117-131   (2nd) 119-132

1. What is the next step in this section that you must do to become a part of the vibrant, fearless Church?

This is where your faith becomes a lifestyle, not a religion. Following Christ means to think like Jesus, say what Jesus would say, do what Jesus would do and treat people the way Jesus treated them. Remember, He treated people like we all would want to be treated. To know how He would react, we must know Him, which means we need to have a personal relationship with Him. The only way you can have a relationship with God is to be righteous. Sin cannot exist where God is. Jesus exchanged His righteousness for your sin. This is why Jesus is the only way to God.

(Romans 3:21-26) **1a** In the verses it says that there is no distinction between all who believe. Why? Jesus was the only human to be perfect.

PROPITIATION: the act of gaining or regaining the favor or goodwill of someone or something. (Merriam-Webster, n.d.) It is interesting to note that the lid of the Ark of the Covenant was called the expiation, the propitiatory. This was where the blood of the sacrificial animal, *the expiatory,* was sprinkled on the annual day of atonement. Jesus became our sacrificial offering, our expiatory for our sins. **EXPIATORY: serving to expiate. EXPIATE:** to make amends for: to extinguish the guilt incurred by; to put an end to.

Jesus served by becoming our Redeemer and made amends for our sins and extinguished the guilt that incurred in us by taking it upon Himself. He put an end to the condemnation for sin. Of course, people must accept that redemption to receive it. People do not automatically get it; they have to receive it by making Jesus the Lord of their lives and living righteously. When they do they have regained God's favor.

If you received Jesus' righteousness, then you need to live righteously and do God's will. You need to be an active Christian. God gets things done on earth through His people; you. You are His mind, heart, love, voice, arms, and legs in this world. You can do this because the power of Holy Spirit is upon you, and you now have eternal life, holy spiritual life.

Many teach that you will receive eternal life when you get to heaven. In a recent conversation with God, He told me that you cannot go to heaven if you do not already have eternal life which comes from Holy Spirit. Living your life like Jesus and representing Him by doing Father God's will is eternal life. It is a spiritual lifestyle here on earth now. That spiritual life will affect the physical things around you.

1b Why can anything in the natural realm, any condition or circumstance, be changed or eliminated by God's Glory?

Eternity supersedes time. **SUPERSEDE: to replace something.**

(Merriam-Webster, 2024)

You receive God's Glory when you receive Holy Spirit. However, it will not manifest into the worldly realm unless you call it forth. However, you must believe Him.

(John 11:40) Jesus believed, and so He raised Lazarus from the dead. He called forth God's glory.

Let us talk about the Glory. God's Glory is His presence. There are three different levels you need to understand. The first one is His omnipresence. His spirit is everywhere all the time. David mentions this:

(Psalm 139:7-10) Since God is everywhere, you do not have to control everything and be everywhere yourself. Trust God.

The second level of Glory is His in-dwelling presence.

(1 Corinthians 3:16) Since Pentecost, when the disciples received Holy Spirit, all believers are filled with Holy Spirit. He gives you eternal life. You have His power and wisdom dwelling in you if you have made Jesus the Lord of your life. Because you are a new spiritual person, Holy Spirit guides you and teaches you God's Truth.

The third level is His manifest presence. This is when Father God personally shows up and acts for a specific purpose, which is known as His Shekinah glory. There are examples in the Bible of God's Shekinah glory. For instance, a burning bush that was not consumed by the fire. (Exodus 3:3-4) Moses was awe struck when he saw this.

Another example is a cloud. (Exodus 13:21-22) Notice that God stayed with them, He never left them alone. Many times, today, people have seen the manifest presence of God as fire, a cloud, or smoke.

This Shekinah Glory is the visible splendor of God. This is when miracles happen, because when Father God shows up, things must conform to His original divine plan. You call forth that manifest glory and declare His will because you believe it!

1c According to the book, what is prayer?

When your spirit is fused with Holy Spirit you are in constant communication with Father God and His supernatural can intervene in the natural realm when you call it forth. However, you must call it forth in faith, believing that which is reality in heaven, can be a reality in the physical realm.

1d Why do God's people keep praying for something that they already have?

Instead of living from the Spirit, they are living *for* the Spirit, which they already have!

If you are truly a follower of Jesus, God is one with you, which means you have the necessary authority to decide against or refuse to accept any of the lies from Satan. You do not have to accept his false reality, his deception. Unfortunately, religion has bought into many of his lies and deception.

2. What is the next step in restoring the Church?

In John 14, Jesus proclaims that He is our Shepherd. **2a** What does the book say you must do to continue to be safe in this world? If you do not know Jesus, you cannot follow Him. **2b** Why? When you get distracted and do not pay attention to Jesus' voice, you will get left behind when He calls His sheep out into the world, and you will be stuck in the sheepfold that day. **2c** According to the book, what does Jesus call the sheepfold?

It is acceptable to gather in the church building, to gain knowledge, to share, to eat together, but you must go into the world, the marketplace, to minister to people. That is your commission as a follower of Jesus; You are an ambassador of heaven. Bring heaven into people's lives, so Jesus can shepherd them. (Psalm 23:2-6) Hearing Jesus' voice is not enough; you must follow Him into the wor.d.

To restate, these are the steps you need to take to become the vibrant Body of Christ:

- Understand how the church was originally set up; Not a religious organization, but a secular one that was open to all people.

- Truly understand what Jesus did for you. Remember, He volunteered.

- Understand the difference between worldly and spiritual, it is critical to your purpose.

- Turn from the worldly ways and repent. When you repent, you give control of your life back to God.

- Do all you can to have a personal relationship with God. It is how you come to know Him.

- Ask for God's help. He has so many blessings to bestow upon you, let Him.

- Study the truth. It is the only way to mature in your faith.

- Stand up to evil. If you do not, you are enabling Satan to carry out his evil plans.

- Be a little Christ to the world. You need to believe IN Jesus; in how He thought, in what He said, in what He did and in how He treated people and then do the same.

- Let Jesus be your shepherd. Trust Him to take you where you need to go. Follow Him.

THINGS TO THINK ABOUT BEFORE THE NEXT STUDY

Which of the ten things listed do I have to work on?

OT (Micah 5:2-5A) [2] But you, O Bethlehem Ephrathah, who are too little to be among the clans of Judah, from you shall come forth for me one who is to be ruler in Israel, whose coming forth is from of old, from ancient days. [3] Therefore he shall give them up until the time when she who is in labor has given birth; then the rest of his brothers shall return to the people of Israel. [4] And he shall stand and shepherd his flock in the strength of the LORD, in the majesty of the name of the LORD his God. And they shall dwell secure, for now he shall be great to the ends of the earth.

[5] And he shall be their peace.

NT (John 10:7-18) [7] So Jesus again said to them, "Truly, truly, I say to you, I am the door of the sheep. [8] All who came before me are thieves and robbers, but the sheep did not listen to them.

[9] I am the door. If anyone enters by me, he will be saved and will go in and out and find pasture. [10] The thief comes only to steal and kill and destroy. I came that they may have life and have it abundantly. [11] I am the good shepherd. The good shepherd lays down his life for the sheep. [12] He who is a hired hand and not a shepherd, who does not own the sheep, sees the wolf coming and leaves the sheep and flees, and the wolf snatches them and scatters them. [13] He flees because he is a hired hand and cares nothing for the sheep. [14] I am the good shepherd. I know my own and my own know me, [15] just as the Father knows me and I know the Father; and I lay down my life for the sheep. [16] And I have other sheep that are not of this fold. (Gentiles) I must bring them also, and they will listen to my voice. So, there will be one flock, one shepherd. [17] For this reason the Father loves me, because I lay down my life that I may take it up again. [18] No

one takes it from me, but I lay it down of my own accord. I have authority to lay it down, and I have authority to take it up again. This charge I have received from my Father.

Meat and Potatoes

(Knowing God)

You are precious to me, Lord.

As you are to me. Look up the meaning of **PRECIOUS. Of great value, not to be wasted or treated carelessly.** (Merriam-Webster, 2024) *What does treat* **carelessly** *mean?* **Done with or acting with insufficient attention; negligent; unconcerned in attitude or action; heedless; indifferent to.** (Merriam-Webster, 2024)

Does that apply to some of my people?

It shouldn't.

I did not ask if it should apply, I asked if it does apply to some.

Yes, Lord, unfortunately it does.

Many who call me precious act as if I am not precious to them. The first description, "of careless treatment," applies to most of my people at some point or another; acting with insufficient attention. Do you agree with that?

Yes, Lord, I do. I can see that just looking at my own life. There are times when I don't pay enough attention to you . . . huh, yet I call You precious. That's sad.

Yes, it is, but at least you are able to recognize your lack of attention and repent and get back on track. Unfortunately, many of my people do not recognize that they are treating me the opposite of what they say I am to them.

Is that because they don't have a personal relationship with you?

Yes, but it is deeper than that. It goes back to what they have been taught, or even to what they have not been taught. They do not know me because they do not realize who I am. Yes, I AM God Almighty, but I yearn for a personal relationship with each one of them. Knowing me, not just knowing about me, is what shows them that I am precious to them, and it is more than just a word to them. It is something that is felt within them, that they truly believe. You truly believe that.

But yet, I don't always treat You like I believe. I'm sorry, Lord.

I know you are, and that is what sets you apart from many of my people. They are not sorry for treating me the opposite of what they call me, because they are not aware that they are treating me that way. They have never really thought about it; Well, after all, I AM God Almighty. I do not have feelings. My heart never breaks . . .

Oh, Lord, I must admit that I believed that at one time, but I don't believe it now.

Why?

Because I know You. I know you have very strong feelings; I know You are precious to me and why You are precious to me. Our relationship is the most important thing in my life!

Mine, too. It is why I sent Yeshua to be the Redeemer.

Study 21 – Dealing With Our Hangups (Part 1)

I wrote in the book that I was frustrated because I was just now learning the things I should have learned as a child. In a more recent conversation, God told me that His Truth was supposed to be passed down from generation to generation. If Jesus' Body had continued to operate as His Ekklesia, it would have been passed down, because it would have been a lifestyle that carried through the generations.

(Psalm 145:4-7;10-13A) **1.** What does verse 13 say?

If you are a parent or will be one, you need to live a lifestyle that honors God. Your children will imitate you because it is your lifestyle. It is not just about having them memorize verses from the Bible or singing songs like *Jesus Loves Me*, but living out life as Jesus would, thinking like Jesus, speaking like Jesus, doing like Jesus, and treating people like Jesus did. (Proverbs 22:6) "Train up a child in the way he should go; even when he is old, he will not depart from it."

Your children will imitate you just as you, as a child of God, should imitate your Father.

(Ephesians 5:1-2) Ask yourself these questions:

2. Am I really a child of God? **3.** Do I imitate my Heavenly Father?

4. Am I walking in love and living out God's Truth in a lifestyle that honors Him? [If it applies] **5.** Am I passing down God's Truth and love to my children and grandchildren?

I, as someone who grew up in church, could not answer yes to most of those questions when God asked me them. I did not know the truth about who I should be as God's child, and how I should be living out my life as a follower of Jesus. I did not realize that my worship, my service, and my ministry should be a lifestyle, not a religion. And most importantly, I did not understand that all this hinges on a personal relationship with God, as His child. I did not know the whole Truth.

PAGES (1st) 132–137   (2nd) 133-138

The book says that our parents and teachers could only teach us what they knew. If they did not understand the whole truth, then they could not pass it down to us. Even though you may not have been taught the truth, God is still going to hold you accountable to live out the truth. **6.** What does the book say you should do?

God wants to save everyone, but you may have some hangups about certain people and will not reach out to them. **7.** What does God want you to understand about that?

8. Who would you consider your enemy? **9.** Do you understand that God loves everyone, including those that you consider enemies? All people were made in God's spiritual image; the same God that made you, made that other person as well.

The book says to remember that God's love is unconditional. **10.**

What is the rest of that sentence say?

11. Why is God able to consider the vilest, most despicable person on earth as worthy to be saved? He separates the person from the deed and then bases the value on that. He can do that because Jesus took our sin upon Himself. Father God does not see sin, but us redeemed. **REDEEMED: freed from captivity by payment of ransom; to be freed from the consequences of sin.**

(King James Bible Online, n.d.-b) (Romans 6:23A) **12.** What is the consequence of sin? Jesus paid our ransom. **Ransom: a sum of money or other payment demanded or paid for the release of a prisoner.**

(Romans 6:20-21) The verse says that as slaves to sin, you were free of righteousness, but you were reaping consequences of sin, which leads to death. Let us see what fruits you were reaping. (Galatians 5:19-21) **13.** List the fruits mentioned. People who have these fruits, these characteristics, are still separated from God, and that is what God says death is; separation from Him.

(Romans 6:23B) **14.** What is the free gift of God?

Let us see what fruits you reap when you have eternal life. (Galatians 5:22-23) When you have these fruits, these characteristics, then you have the characteristics of God. You have accepted Jesus' redemption and have made Jesus the Lord of your life. There is no law against these things, although a ruler or government may try to make a law against these things, but God says, "No!"

(Galatians 5:24-25) **15.** What have those who belong to Christ Jesus done? **16.** If you live by the Spirit, then what should you do?

Let Holy Spirit direct your life. If you do, you will see things, circumstances, and others through God's eyes. In the book, God talks about "enemies." He says that people are not His enemies.

17. Write down what Romans 5:10 says.

RECONCILE: to restore to friendship or harmony. (Merriam-Webster, 2024) **18.** If you are a friend, then what are you not?

19. Were you saved when Jesus reconciled you through His death?

20. How were you saved?

Remember, Jesus gave you the right for eternal life, but it is your choice to make Him Lord of your life and to do Father God's will. That is when you get eternal life, when the Holy Spirit is in you and guiding you. **21.** What does God say about those who do not accept redemption? **22.** What are the two summaries God gives about this topic? [In this regard, fear means to be afraid of.]

(Galatians 3:25-29) **23.** If you are in Christ, you are Abraham's offspring, and what else? **24.** Have you put on Christ? **25.** Are you a part of the Body of Christ? **26.** Are you being His mind, voice, arms, and legs in this worldly realm? **27.** How? **28.** Do people see Jesus in your life, or do they only see you or something else?

The book says God wants you to understand that humans are not His enemies. **29.** Who is? He is the enemy within, and He needs to be replaced with God.

God says in the book that if you think people are His enemies then you will let them fall into eternity without Him. That is not what He wants!

Eternity will not end, so every person will be in eternity because they are spirit, they do not stop existing when they suffer a physical death. They will exist in eternal death (eternal separation from God) or eternal life with God. Each person makes that choice for themselves.

THINGS TO THINK ABOUT BEFORE THE NEXT STUDY

Who have I assumed God did not think of as worthy to be saved? Why did I think that?

OT (Ezekiel 33:10-11) [10] "And you, son of man, say to the house of Israel, thus have you said: 'Surely our transgressions and our sins are upon us, and we rot away because of them. How then can we live?' [11] Say to them, As I live, declares the Lord GOD, I have no pleasure in the death of the wicked, but that the wicked turn from his way and live; turn back, turn back from your evil ways, for why will you die, O house of Israel?

NT (John 3:16-17) [16] "For God so loved the world, that he gave his only begotten Son, that whoever believes in him should not perish but have eternal life. [17] For God did not send his Son into the world to condemn the world, but in order that the world might be saved through him.

Meat and Potatoes

(Honored to be our Father)

You are such an amazing and wondrous God; I am honored and grateful to be a part of Your family.

I am honored to be your Father, as Yeshua is honored to be your brother, and Holy Spirit is honored to be your connection to and representative of our kingdom. We do not take being God lightly; it is a big responsibility. What is most important to us is knowing our creation and having a personal relationship with all people.

We are not just all powerful, out in space somewhere, we are also close to each part of our creation. We know everything about it, and can name each part, each animal, and every person. We love and care for our whole creation, especially each human conceived, or will be conceived.

We do not look at you as 'subjects,' which is what most people think. We see you as beloved, cherished individuals. And we want all of you to be a part of our family. (Smiling) We do not just sit back and hope that will happen, we do everything we can to make it happen, because we love and cherish you all.

Every one of you are precious to us. I say to you all, "Come. Be a part of our family. It would be my honor to be your Father. Shalom."

Study 22 – Dealing with Our Hangups (Parts 2-3)

As God was telling me about His feelings concerning enemies, I realized I had never learned most of this before, but I should not be surprised since Satan has infiltrated the churches. He does not want people to be saved, which means he does not want God's people to know how God feels about who is and who is not the enemy.

Pages (1st) 137-145   (2nd) 138-143

In this part 2, God asked me what the main theme is in the Old Testament when it mentions enemies. **1.** What was the answer?

2. Why did God consider them enemies to His people? **3.** Why did the people have to call on God to defeat their enemies? **4.** What happened when God's people went into battle without calling on Him first?

God says that He is the same now, before, and forever, so if people are not His enemies now, they were not then. On the previous page He said they were the enemies of His people, not His. I asked Him why He destroyed those people if they were not His enemies. **5.** What was His answer?

He could not let that happen because He loves all people. He does not want them to spend eternity without Him. He said He would not have needed to destroy anyone if His people had just done His will from the beginning.

6. Why could someone be an enemy to God's people without being an enemy to Him?

Of course, destroyed means to suffer physical death, but when God mentions died in this sentence, it means spiritual death; eternal separation from Him. God is spirit, so death has no hold on Him. Enemies steal, kill, and destroy. God cannot be destroyed because He is the Creator. The created cannot destroy the Creator. God said He did not implant the desire to steal, kill, and destroy into humans when He made them. **7.** Where did those actions come from?

God created everyone and knows everything about us. (Matthew 10:29-31) **8.** Why does verse 31 say you should not be afraid? People may try and hide something from others or themselves, but they cannot hide anything from God. There is no place that a person can go that God is not already there. He is omnipresent.

(Hebrews 4:12-13) **9.** What does verse 13 say you will have to do?

10. What will you say when He asks, "Why?"

At one point in our conversation, the atmosphere changed, and I knew that God was speaking as God the Almighty instead of God the Father when He said that every person conceived has a purpose. Each person has a book written about everything God has ordained for them. (Psalm 139:16) **11.** When was your book written?

12. How many people will Satan lie to, to get them to believe that some people do not matter? **13.** Who matters to God?

The topic of abortion is not about being pro-abortion or pro-life. It is about babies being born so they will be able to carry out the purposes God has ordained for them, just as you have a purpose God ordained for you. **14** What did God say about His babies' lives being cut short and their destinies cut off?

15. Since the death and resurrection of Jesus, who are the enemies of God's people? (Ephesians 6:12) **16.** Where are the spiritual forces of evil from? This verse explains that your enemies are not from the physical realm. That is, of course, if you are a child of God. If you are not a child of God, humans can be your enemies because they could kill your body, and you would spend eternity in hell. Of course, those people are being controlled by or influenced by Satan.

17. Why does the book say that sometimes God's people think of humans as their enemies? Remember that the spirit has authority over the physical things if we are living from the Spirit. **18.** Why do God's people have no human enemies? Remember, it is a spiritual battle we are fighting.

God is telling His Ekklesia to come out of Babylon. Babylon was the name of the city that was considered very evil, the people worshipped many gods there. In the ancient times it was where the Tower of Babel was. Babylon is also the word used to represent the worldly systems influenced by Satan. These systems are spoken of in Isaiah and Revelation concerning the day of the Lord when He comes back to rule.

(Isaiah 2:6-22) **19.** What will the people do when Jesus shows up again on earth to rule? (It is mentioned twice in the verses.)

Notice verse 22 says to stop looking at humankind-controlled systems to take care of you. Man is created, not the Creator that breathed breath into man's nostrils. This is the Satan influenced, greedy, global financial system that controls global markets and industries, self-centered governments, and false religions.

(Revelation 18:1-3) God is telling about the fall of the demonic world system. (Revelation 18:4-5) Stop living from the worldly system and live from God's heavenly system. You are supposed to be an ambassador for heaven, so live from the Spirit, not for the Spirit. You have been ordained to take God's Good News into the world so that people can see the Truth and choose God. You can only do that if you know that each person is loved and valued by God.

Part 3: The book says that in the Bible the word from which enemy is translated from, means to hate. The definition is hated, odious, hateful, and hostile, opposing another. **20.** What does God say can happen with any human at any given time?

If a person directs their life from the carnal mind, including a child of God, they have a huge opportunity to oppose God. They are vulnerable to Satan's lies and snares that he sets. God says this happens to His people often. **21.** Does He call them the enemy?

22. What does He call them? They must repent and turn back to God, though.

God says that Jesus is done with the aggravating lukewarmness. He is going to concentrate on the remnant (Ekklesia) and the new generation.

(Revelation 3:16) **23.** What does this verse say about God's people that are sitting on the fence waiting for something to happen, not being active Christians by not doing His will?

24. According to the book, which people are cold, because they do not have the fire of God inside them? **25.** Which type of person is hot? **26.** Why are the carnal people lukewarm?

27. Are you lukewarm? **28.** Is there a chance that Jesus is going to spit you out? **29.** If yes, why? God needs you to take your authority back as part of His Ekklesia and fulfill your destiny.

THINGS TO THINK ABOUT BEFORE THE NEXT STUDY

What worldly systems do I put my trust in before God?

OT (Proverbs 3:1-12) [1] My son, do not forget my teaching, but let your heart keep my commandments, [2] for length of days and years of life and peace they will add to you. [3] Let not steadfast love and faithfulness forsake you; bind them around your neck; write them on the tablet of your heart. [4] So you will find favor and good success in the sight of God and man. [5] Trust in the LORD with all your heart, and do not lean on your own understanding. [6] In all your ways acknowledge him, and he will make straight your paths. [7] Be not wise in your own eyes; fear the LORD and turn away from evil. [8] It will be healing to your flesh and refreshment to your bones. [9] Honor the LORD with your wealth and with the first fruits of all your produce; [10] then your barns will be filled with plenty, and your vats will be bursting with wine. [11] My son, do not despise the LORD's discipline or be weary of his reproof,

[12] for the LORD reproves him whom he loves, as a father the son in whom he delights.

NT (Romans 8:5-9) [5] For those who live according to the flesh set their minds on the things of the flesh, but those who live according to the Spirit set their minds on the things of the Spirit.

[6] For to set the mind on the flesh is death, but to set the mind on the Spirit is life and peace. [7] For the mind that is set on the flesh is hostile to God, for it does not submit to God's law; indeed, it cannot. [8] Those who are in the flesh cannot please God. [9] You, however, are not in the flesh but in the Spirit, if in fact the Spirit of God dwells in you. Anyone who does not have the Spirit of Christ does not belong to him.

Meat and Potatoes

(God rebukes for change)

I went into a vision where I was sitting with God in heaven.

I called you up here. Do you know why?

Yes. You want me to convey a personal message to someone. I am hesitant to do so because it is a tough love message.

Yes, it is.

(Sighing) I have to do your will.

You do not have to. I will not force you.

(Sighing) I committed to You, so I really don't have a choice. That's what my heart says. Okay. What's your message?

This message is for a certain person, but parts of it are also a message for all my people, so write it down in your journal. You will send a separate note to the individual. First, I have a question for you: Do you understand that I sometimes rebuke my people because I love them and want the best for them?

Yes Abba . . . Why would You even ask me that?

Because many of my people do not really believe that. They think I am angry and want to punish them. I asked you that question because you would not be able to deliver my message if you did not believe that I rebuke my people because I care for them. I want the best for them. I want them to have abundant life on earth right now. But that will not happen if they are not representing me. And if not me, then guess who they are representing.

Look up the word REBUKE. **To reprimand; strongly warn; restrain.** (Merriam-Webster, 2024)

What is the meaning of REPRIMAND? **An official rebuke.** (Merriam-Webster, 2024) *I officially rebuke someone as God Almighty.*

Strongly warn means to strongly advise someone to do or not to do something in order to avoid danger or punishment. *(Merriam-Webster,2024) I strongly warn people as Father God because I love them and do not want them to suffer because of danger or punishment.*

What is the meaning of RESTRAIN? **1. Prevent (someone or something) from doing something; keep under control or within limits. 2. Prevent (oneself) from displaying or giving way to (a strong urge or emotion) 3. Deprive (someone) of freedom of movement or personal liberty.** (Definitions C Meaning/Britannica Dictionary, n.d.)

I do not rebuke to deprive someone of freedom of movement or personal liberty. I do it to call to their attention what is happening, so that they can prevent themselves from displaying or giving way to strong urges or emotions. When my people give way to those things, they have turned down their switches to my power, to my Holy Spirit. They are not representing me or my kingdom at that point; they are representing Satan and his kingdom. I rebuke my people to remind them of how important it is to control themselves so that they can stay within the limits I have set for them. These are carnal limits so that my people can represent my kingdom here on earth. You are my children; you need to act like it. If you go beyond the limits I have set, then you are representing the kingdom of Satan, the kingdom of the world, the kingdom of darkness and death.

I love you, my people, but you must understand that I love all people and want to spend eternity with them as well. If you are not acting as my ambassadors, you are not representing my kingdom, and as a result, others will not have a chance to know me and to understand that they can have eternal life with me. This is not acceptable to me! I love! It is who I AM! You are my voice, my arms, and legs in the physical realm. I cannot tell people how much I love them because they have no spiritual connection to me. I cannot show them how much I love them; you must do it for me.

Galatians 5:22-23 lists the fruit of the Spirit, the last one being self-control. These spiritual fruits should be seen by others in your lives. These are my traits, and Jesus' traits, and should be your traits, not the least of which is self-control. I want you to inherit all that my kingdom offers. I rebuke you so that you can be aware of who you are representing. If it is not me, then my rebuke is a reminder to repent and get back on track doing my will.

Study 23 – The Fear Factor

You may have some hangups, but so do others.

PAGES (1st)145 – 155   (2nd) 145-155

1. List the four reasons given that may keep people from turning to God, and the reason they feel that way.

WIMPY: not strong, brave, or confident. (Merriam-Webster, 2024)

2. Are you strong in your faith? **3.** Are you brave enough to stand up for God's truth? **4.** Do you have confidence in your relationship with God? **5.** Have you been a poor example of God? Jesus was the perfect example of God.

(John 14:9) **6.** What did Jesus tell His disciples about Himself? Jesus conducted Himself in a way that brought glory to Father God, because He acted according to the will and authority of Father God. That is what you must do. You conduct yourself under the authority that Jesus has given to you, as His follower, thinking, speaking, doing, and treating people the way Jesus would. You do all those things in Jesus' name, in other words, on His behalf. When you do something in Jesus' name, that means you are acting according to the will and authority of Jesus, on His behalf.

(John 14:12-14) **7.** According to the verse, if you ask Jesus anything in His name, what will He do?

Jesus is not just telling the disciples to end their prayers with, "In Jesus' name I pray, amen." He is telling them to pray with His authority, on behalf of Him. You have taken His name-- Christian, Christlike, follower of Jesus-- you are now operating in His name, as His representative. You now have authority to petition God in

Jesus' name, as His follower, because you are thinking like Jesus, talking like Jesus, doing things like Jesus, and treating people like Jesus did. You are following His principles, His commandments.

Think of police officers who may tell you to stop in the name of the law, which is the authority under which they are operating. We declare in the name of Jesus, who is our authority that we operate under.

8. Do people see Jesus in you when they look at you and your life? If you do not act with authority against the worldly things, you cannot change anything. Remember, you are an ambassador of heaven. You have the authority to act on the behalf of Jesus (2 Corinthians 5:20) **9.** How are you to implore?

You are here for a purpose. Do not sit back and do nothing! (James 1:22-25) **10.** What does the verse say about those that are doers and not just hearers?

You will be blessed because you have made a difference in someone's life, because of your example. Father God blessed Jesus when He made a difference in your life, and Jesus will bless you when you make a difference in someone else's life.

Whatever you do in Jesus' name, under His authority, God will bless it. You must make a decision to live out the truth like Jesus did. Remember, it is a lifestyle, living like Jesus.

(Romans 12:1-2) **11.** How are you transformed from being conformed to the world? If you live by your desires and emotions, your life is like those in the world. As a result, you suffer the consequences, and you are very vulnerable to Satan's lies and deceit. The more you operate in the carnal, the farther away from God you get. If your life looks like unbelievers' lives, they will not give their lives over to Jesus when you tell them that Jesus will set them free. If your life is no different than theirs, what is the point?

They will wonder what Jesus set you free from. They do not see any difference. **12.** Is your life different than theirs?

13. Why do you think people fear God? I asked the Lord, "Who wants to have a relationship with someone who instills fear in them?" We had a conversation about that. The next questions are based on that conversation.

14. When the Lord asked me why I was not afraid to be with Him, what was my answer?

He said to imagine that I was someone who did not know Him and that I would be afraid because I would not understand who He was. This is why you need a personal relationship with God. To understand Him you must know Him.

15. According to the book, how long did it take for Adam and Eve to suffer the consequences of sin? (Genesis 3:6-7) **16.** What was the first consequence they suffered after sinning? (Genesis 3:8-10) **17.** What was the second consequence of sinning? (Genesis 3:11-13) **18.** What was the third consequence of sin for Adam?

This is a quite common consequence, not holding oneself accountable for what one does, making excuses.**19.** Do you hold yourself accountable when you are not living like you should, or do you make excuses and if so, what are they?

20. According to the book, why didn't God send the Messiah immediately? This was so people would know that He was the promised one. God decreed that all who would accept His Son as Redeemer and Lord, could have a relationship with Him again. **21.** When that happens, what does God's perfect love do according to 1 John 4:18? Fear has to do with punishment, and whoever fears has not been perfected in God's love. Stay in God's love so you need not fear.

22. When will people give their lives to Jesus? **23.** What must you have to be able to finish the work that God has ordained for you to do? **24.** What sets you apart from the rest of the world?

The book says that God's people are not afraid of Him because His perfect love is in them. **25.** What is the big IF? **26.** Why is God's Church, the Body of Christ, not seeing any results when they try and minister?

You can only know God's will for you through a personal, spiritual relationship with Him.

27. What is the wrong approach to ministering? **28.** What is the correct approach to ministering?

God referenced a verse (2 Chronicles 7:14) "If my people who are called by my name humble themselves and pray and seek my face and turn from their wicked ways, then I will hear from heaven and will forgive their sin and heal their land."

Wake up Church! Turn your switch back ON. Do it now. Time is very short!

THINGS TO THINK ABOUT BEFORE THE NEXT STUDY

Do I need to humble myself, pray and seek God more and turn from some wicked ways?

How so?

OT (Isaiah 55:6-9) [6] Seek the LORD while he may be found; call upon him while he is near; [7] let the wicked forsake his way, and the unrighteous man his thoughts; let him return to the LORD, that he may have compassion on him, and to our God, for he will abundantly pardon. [8] For my thoughts are not your thoughts, neither are your ways my ways, declares the LORD. [9] For as the heavens are higher than the earth, so are my ways higher than your ways and my thoughts than your thoughts.

NT (Philippians 2:14-16) [14] Do all things without grumbling or disputing, [15] that you may be blameless and innocent, children of God without blemish in the midst of a crooked and twisted generation, among whom you shine as lights in the world, [16] holding fast to the word of life, so that in the day of Christ I may be proud that I did not run in vain or labor in vain.

Meat and Potatoes

(Many Prophesies)

You know what's really sad? That there were hundreds of prophesies about the Messiah, enough so that only one person could fulfill them all. This was so that there would be no doubt that You were the Messiah.

Yes . . . No doubt . . .

But the very people who knew all the prophesies are the ones that doubted the most, the religious leaders.

Yes, blinded from the Truth by Satan's deceit, and their selfish ambition and greed, and their power, prestige, and conceit.

There was absolutely no other person that fulfilled all the prophecies.

Not a one.

Then it should have been clear to them.

Yes, it should have been perfectly clear, just as it should be perfectly clear now.

Huh. You've fulfilled even more of the prophesies since your death, resurrection, and ascension back to heaven.

And soon I will fulfill another prophesy. Do you know what it is?

You coming back to take your people out of the earth.

Can you think of any other prophesies that I have yet to fulfill?

You will come back and conquer Satan's army, and you will reign as King over the earth. Also, You will be judge over all the people at the White Thrown Judgement.

Let me ask you a question: Will there ever come a time when all people will believe that I am Messiah?

Yes, at judgement: every knee shall bow, and every voice shall confess that You are who You say you are.

Write down the verse that pertains to that.

Philippians 2:10 – so at the name of Jesus every knee shall bow, in heaven and on earth and under the earth, and every tongue confess that Jesus Christ is Lord, to the glory of God.

Study 24 – Important Messages to Understand and Pass On

There are certain issues that we must understand and then let others know why God considers them important.

PAGES (1st) 155–167   (2nd) 155-167

There are three issues God mentions in this section, the first being the sacrifice of our children. **1.** Why will Satan do everything imaginable to wipe out these precious children?

I told Jesus that I was grateful to Him for loving the children in heaven and showing them how important, beautiful, and wanted they are. **2.** What did Father God say about them besides mentioning that they are precious to Him?

This is another reason Satan wants to wipe the children out; he knows it brings anguish to God because they are so precious to Him.

3. What was the vision I had of Jesus and the children? He loves the children so much. (Mark 10:13-16) **4.** In those verses what does Jesus say you must do to enter the kingdom of heaven? There is a blessing. (Mark 9:36-37) **5.** If you receive a child in Jesus' name, what else do you receive?

Receiving God means entering the kingdom of heaven, but there is an IF. (Matthew 18:1-4) **6.** What is the reason that Jesus says you will not enter the kingdom of heaven? **7.** What do you think that means?

(Matthew 18:5-6) **8.** What did Jesus say would be better for someone to do if there is a chance for that person to cause a child to sin? It would be a better outcome for that person than it would be if that person harms a child and goes to hell.

9. In His message to the people who had an abortion, what are the four important things God mentioned about those aborted children? God wants the parents to give the children their desires.

10. What must they do to accomplish that?

God wants them to choose life and live with Him in eternity so they can meet their children again and He says it will be a glorious reunion. You who have lost young ones to disease, accidents and murder have the same opportunity to meet your children again, as well!

The second issue God mentions in this section is the collapse of the family. He wants people to value the family. **11.** What is one of the most devastating outcomes of any of Satan's attacks? God wants the honoring of families restored.**12.** Why does Satan want families to be destroyed?

13. In the dream about buildings and people, what does the ground represent? **14.** What does the smaller building represent? **15.** What does the large building represent?

These are governmental controlled dwellings.**16.** What do the people in charge of the dwelling, the agents of the building's owner, represent? **17.** Who does the owner represent?

God ordained the family so there is protection and provision for children as they grow. Parents are not only to provide for the young, but to teach them as well. (Proverbs 22:6) **18.** If you train up a child in the way he should go, what will happen when the child is old?

Remember, God said before that His Truth was supposed to be passed down from generation to generation. As you can see, Satan has stopped that by destroying the family institution. Families are to be representative of God's family and His care for us. Satan cannot have that.

19. When does Satan have an open doorway of access to a family?

20. What is Satan doing through his "agents"? This means that people will have to depend on governments to take care of them.

21. What security is provided by good families as listed in the book? (1 Corinthians 13:4-8A) **22.** When will unconditional love end?

23. What would happen if more people are dependent on the system than are working to supply funds needed? This is what happens when worldly (human) solutions are used to try and solve worldly problems, instead of using spiritual solutions.

24. When can we develop strong family units, with unselfish desires to help each other and trust God's ability to take care of us? We, God's children, *you*, need to set the example.

Jesus told me that there was a great celebration when I joined the family of God. I was astonished. I asked Him why it is so hard for us to see ourselves as He sees us. **25.** What was Father God's answer?

The third issue that God wants us to understand is why the Church needs to wake up. **26.** According to the book, why does God need His Church to wake up? He says His Church has been silent too long. **27.** Why did God ordain WAKE UP CHURCH! to be written?

28. What is the root of all the immoral behavior in today's world? We are in a battle, and we must be prepared and wearing God's armor. **29.** Write down what each piece of armor represents.

Belt:

Breastplate:

Shoes:

Shield:

Helmet:

Sword of the Spirit:

As long as you gird yourself with these things, no one can overcome you. (Isaiah 54:17) **30.** What does it say about any weapon Satan may use against you?

31. How big is that swamp that God is helping His Ekklesia to drain? God says that our victory is not going to happen overnight, it is going to take stealth and cunning like never before in history. You must trust God and do your part, knowing God loves all people.

32. What are we supposed to let them know?

33. Why is this not an easy battle? Remember, we are not strong enough to fight the enemy in the natural realm. We must fight him in the spiritual realm because we have the power from Holy Spirit. **34.** Why are many of God's people trying to fight from the natural, physical realm?

35. What is this huge battle over the souls of humankind all about?

36. How long should we pray?

THINGS TO THINK ABOUT BEFORE THE NEXT STUDY

Am I showing God's unconditional love to my family? How?

OT (Proverbs 20:7) The righteous who walks in his integrity—blessed are his children after him!

NT (Colossians 3:12-17) [12] Put on then, as God's chosen ones, holy and beloved, compassionate hearts, kindness, humility, meekness, and patience, [13] bearing with one another and, if one has a complaint against another, forgiving each other; as the Lord has forgiven you, so you also must forgive. [14] And above all these, put on love, which binds everything together in perfect harmony. [15] And let the peace of Christ rule in your hearts, to which indeed you were called in one body. And be thankful. [16] Let the word of Christ dwell in you richly, teaching and admonishing one another in all wisdom, singing psalms and hymns and spiritual songs, with thankfulness in your hearts to God. [17] And whatever you do, in word or deed, do everything in the name of the Lord Jesus, giving thanks to God the Father through him.

Meat and Potatoes

(Age of understanding)

You, as a spiritual being, do not need a body to exist. However, you do need a body to interact in the world. When you are physically born your spirits are disconnected from my Spirit, which means your spirits are dead because there is no connection to the Spirit of Life.

When you believe that Jesus is your Redeemer (he died in your place) and rose from the dead (he is alive), and you have accepted Him as your Savior and Lord, you are connected to me through my Spirit of Life. This is a choice that each person makes. Each decides if they will spend eternity with me or without me. The only exceptions are those that do not have the mental ability to make that choice, like young children and someone who is mentally underdeveloped and is incapable of discerning the truth.

What age is that?

It depends on the child.

But the parents don't know when that will be.

That is why it is imperative that they teach their children the Truth from the beginning.

They can't teach newborns; they don't understand language.

True, but they can declare the Truth and decree it over their children. Decree it every day and it will begin to sink in as the child develops. Then when the child is developed enough to understand, the parents begin teaching them my Word, my Truth.

What if the parents don't know the Truth?

A better question would be about why they do not know the Truth.

Ah . . . Your Church is not living out the Truth?

Uh huh. But after the age of accountability is reached, each person must seek the Truth for themselves, for they will be held accountable for their own actions and decisions.

But if they never know the Truth and "die," they will be separated from You for all eternity.

If they never sought and accepted Yeshua, yes.

That doesn't seem fair.

Well, I want them to spend eternity with me, and I want to tell them that, but how do I do that when I do not have a physical voice?

(Sighing) Through your Church.

Yes, through my Ekklesia, not just with words, but through their examples as thy live my Truth. It is a lifestyle.

So, we are accountable.

Well, you are accountable for not being who I created you to be or not doing what I created you to do. However, I put inside each person a desire to know me. It is up to each person to fulfill that desire. They know I AM, but most spend their entire lives trying to convince themselves that I do not exist.

If people say they do not believe there is a God, then why do most of them look for proof that You do not exist? If they truly believed what they say, wouldn't they look for proof that you *do* exist?

(Smiling) That is a very good question.

Study 25 – The Ekklesia – Special Forces

We are fighting a spiritual battle, and God needs every soldier of His Ekklesia awake, and on active duty.

PAGES (1st) 167-173   (2nd) 167-173

If we are fighting a battle, we need a battle plan. However, you must understand something before you can fight.

(2 Corinthians 10:3-5) **1.** In those verses it says that our weapons are not of the flesh, but what do they have?

STRONGHOLD: a building or position that is strongly defended. A place or area where a particular belief or activity is common. (Merriam-Webster, 2024)

Satan strongly defends his position in people's lives, and he will do anything necessary to keep people focused on a particular belief or activity so that they never see the truth and are freed from his deceit. Your weapons have the power to do that very thing: to destroy his lies and free people.

2. What is the main mission of the Ekklesia?

False realities are what Satan deceives people with. To understand what unreconciled means, remember the meaning of **RECONCILE: to restore to friendship or harmony.** In our case it means friendship and harmony with God and each other. Remember, Jesus came to unite us. If someone is in harmony with God, then they can know the truth, the real reality.

There are six false realities that must be reconciled. **3.** What are they?

These are the battlegrounds. You can read about them in Ephesians.

4. According to the book, who is the Supreme Commander? **5.** Who is the commander in chief?

6. What are the four things to do to carry out your mission? **7.** How close are the people to the kingdom of God when you minister to them?

These are the things that Jesus and His disciples did. Jesus showed them how to do things. He still does. He is not back at Command Central; He is fighting alongside of us.

As part of the Ekklesia Special Forces, we are to go behind enemy lines and seize his territory and clear it out. **8.** Where does the book say the enemy territory is? **9.** Why is Satan's territory a swamp?

We, as the Ekklesia, must bring that Living Water into the swamp. We do not do that with certain programs or projects, we do it with a trans-cultural, trans-generational, and trans-denominational lifestyle. It is a lifestyle that overcomes multiple cultures, multiple generations, and multiple denominations. In other words, it unites us all in common harmony, with God and each other, through spiritual principles, not with any programs or projects in the physical realm.

Jesus understood the Ekklesia's mission had to be based on holy principles, because the physical realm has restrictions, and He wants all people to have access to His kingdom. **10.** In His kingdom who is welcomed and equal?

The method the Ekklesia uses to build the spiritual channel that brings the Living Water into the swamp is a two-fold method that builds the banks of the channel. Write down what must be done to fulfill each paradigm. **PARADIGM: a typical example or pattern of something; a model.** (Merriam-Webster, 2024)

11. The WHAT:

12. The WHY:

ATONEMENT: Reparation (making amends for) a wrong (sins or an injury). (Merriam-Webster, 2024) It is the reconciliation (restoring friendly relations) with God and humankind through Jesus Christ. The marketplace is essentially where the life of a community is centered: the public.

13. The HOW:

14. The WHERE:

15. The WHAT FOR:

Until Adam and Eve sinned, there was no poverty, humans had everything they needed. As soon as they sinned poverty began, because instead of relying on Holy Spirit, they now had to rely on themselves, on their own abilities to get the things needed to live a physical life. Our human abilities are quite pitiful compared to God's abilities.

Poverty was the first tangible manifestation of the gates of hell on earth. **MANIFESTATION: an event, action or object that clearly shows or embodies something.** (Merriam-Webster, 2024) That which happened in the spiritual realm that you could not see, (separation from God), caused a tangible change in the physical realm. (Humans had to work the land for their food and make everything they needed.)

16. What makes up the second bank of the channel?

Prayer helps change things in the spiritual realm. You must change the spiritual climate in a nation, or town, or neighborhood, family before some physical things can change.

(Ephesians 3:7-12) The mystery spoken of in these verses was hidden until Paul became a follower of Jesus. He was given the responsibility of opening up the kingdom of God to all people, not just the Jews. It is through this awesome, worldwide, unified Body of Christ that God's wisdom is manifested and then seen by the rulers and authorities in the spiritual realm. Remember, you are fighting against evil spiritual entities, so those must be bound or removed so that people are no longer influenced by them and now can see the Truth that sets them free. That is possible now because the spiritual entities realize that God's people have the wisdom and authority over the spiritual realm that they did not have before Jesus redeemed them. Do not forget, you are to live out a lifestyle of prayer and evangelism, just as Jesus did.

Now, something needs to be set straight. There are those who say women cannot be evangelists or prophets because they would be teaching men. But, be assured, that is not the case, as the following scriptures show:

(2 Kings 22:14-16) Here, God directed a woman to give a prophetic message, from Him, to a man who was a king.

(Exodus 15:20) Aaron's sister was a prophet.

Anna was a prophet when Jesus was a child and when she saw Him, she spoke of Him as the Redeemer. (Luke 2:36-38) **17.** Who did Anna speak to about Jesus as the Messiah?

According to different dictionaries**: PROPHET: a person who is sent by God to teach people and give them messages from God; a person regarded as an inspired teacher or proclaimer**

of the will of God; a person who predicts the future. (Merriam-Webster, 2024)

Look at the definition of **EVANGELIZE: to preach the Gospel.** (Merriam-Webster, n.d.) The Gospel is about Jesus and what He came to earth to do. The first person to evangelize that Jesus was the Messiah, was the woman at the well. She was the first person that Jesus publicly told He was the Messiah. (John 4:7) He talks to her about how He is the Living Water. (John 4:10-15)

(John 4:16-18) Jesus told the woman something about herself that He could not have known. **18.** What was it?

(John 4:19-26) They talked about where people worshipped God and Jesus told her that the hour has come when the true worshippers would worship God in spirit and truth. She went and told others about Jesus. (John 4:28-29) **19.** What was the question she asked the people?

The first person to evangelize about Jesus rising from the dead (coming back to life) was a woman. (John 20:16-18) **20.** What did she tell the disciples?

All of God's people should be evangelizing, if not in words, then in actions.

THINGS TO THINK ABOUT BEFORE THE NEXT STUDY

Am I treating what I do (whether it is cleaning a house, working a job, being a parent or going to school, etc.) as worship to God? If not, what can I do to improve that?

How would that change my way of thinking about what I do and how I do things?

OT (Proverbs 16:3) Commit your work to the LORD, and your plans will be established.

NT (Colossians 3:23-24) [23] Whatever you do, work heartily, as for the Lord and not for men, [24] knowing that from the Lord you will receive the inheritance as your reward. You are serving the Lord Christ.

Meat and Potatoes

(Time vs Eternity)

Do not forget that you are an ambassador of heaven now, and you live in eternity and are not bound by time. Therefore, live a supernatural life, an abundant life, a joyous life, and a productive life. If you treat everything you do as worship to me, you will be amazed at what you can accomplish. Do not focus on time, focus on me, and take the word "time" out of your vocabulary. Instead of saying, "I do not think I have time to do this," say, "I will get this done because it is God's will. I do not have to calculate this or worry about that, because Holy Spirit will guide me, and I am going to focus on Your will, Lord." When you stop focusing on time, and change your attitude about it, you will be amazed at what you can accomplish. Do I worry about time? No, neither should you, just focus on me and do my will. Every day get up and ask Holy Spirit what is on the agenda for today, he will tell you throughout the day.

I know how awesome you are. I created you, and I do not make mistakes, so live the abundant life I planned for you. Focus on me, my will, my Truth, and stop focusing on temporary things like time. Time is temporary, eternity is not. You are my child and do not have to wait on time to get your blessings, they are all available to you right now. My blessings supersede anything in the natural realm, including time. Just go for it, and do not worry. I will take care of you because I love you. Trust me. Remember, with me nothing is too hard, and nothing is impossible, if it is my will, part of my divine plan.

Study 26 – Encouraging Words

Our fight can be tough at times because Satan is not going to just roll over and give up, but God has promised to take care of us. As long as we keep our eyes on Jesus and trust Holy Spirit to guide us, we can and will prevail. Let God encourage you.

Pages (1st) 173-185   (2nd) 173-184

In the verse shown in the book (Isaiah 41:10) God says to fear not. **1.** Why? **2.** Why should you not be dismayed? **3.** What does it say He will do?

4. What does Psalms 46:1 say? He will never ever abandon you.

5. Have you ever abandoned God?

6. In David's Song, what does he say the Lord saves him from?

7. It says that the Lord has recompensed David according to what?

8. Is your righteousness based on what you have done? **9.** If no, what is it based on? **10.** If yes, what are the works that make you righteous? (Galatians 2:16)

11. In the book, David says that the Lord is his lamp, and what does it do? **12.** To whom is the Lord a shield? **13.** For what does the Lord train us?

You must be like-minded with Jesus. **14.** List eight things that Jesus did while here on earth.

These are the things we should be focusing on and doing, just like Jesus did. **15.** Do you think you would be able to do these things if you had to rely on your carnal mind and not on Holy Spirit, through your spiritual mind? **16.** Why?

All these things that Jesus did was to help and bless others. He treated everyone with respect and compassion, except when He was rebuking the religious leaders. **17.** It is obvious that Jesus treated people like we all want to be treated, so why do you think so many people hate Him?

Part of taking care of you is protecting you. Psalms 91 is a two-part protection plan, that God has given to us. When in peril, danger, or despair, recite this Psalm as a prayer to God.

18. What does the Psalm say God delivers you from? The trapper is Satan, and he knows exactly the right places to put his traps to ensnare you. **19.** Who does God charge to guard you in your ways?

20. What are the three responsibilities you have in this protection plan? **21.** What are the two things that are God's responsibilities?

22. What are the benefits of this protection? **23.** What four things will you not be afraid of?

24. What three things happen when you put your trust in God? These are five of the promises God gives to you: He will deliver you; He sits you on high with Him and Jesus, He will answer you when you call out to Him, He will be with you when you are in trouble, He will deliver you from that trouble.

I have personally experienced this supernatural protection. My husband and I were riding a motorcycle and went down due to a rainy wet road. We skidded on our side into an intersection as two cars were approaching from two other directions. We were all going to hit the intersection at the same time. When the bike stopped skidding, in the middle of the intersection, I looked around and could not see either of the two cars. They were gone. I believe that angels picked them up and moved them past the intersection down the road in the direction they were headed. What an awesome God we serve!

25. What supernatural protection was provided in the narrative about the motorcycle?

26. According to the book, what are the other three promises God makes to you if you love Him?

27. According to Isaiah 54:17 what is the heritage of the servants of the Lord, and His vindication?

You can refute because Holy Spirit will speak for you **REFUTE: to say or prove that a person, statement, opinion, etc. is wrong or false.** (Definitions C Meanings/Britannica Dictionary, n.d.) . (Matthew 10:19-20)

As a child of God, when someone accuses you, they are usually speaking lies, or they have false information, or a misguided belief of what is true. Holy Spirit will set them straight if you trust in Him to do so. He will give you the words to say.

28. In the message to non-believers what is the first thing that God said? (1 Samuel 16:7) He knows your heart. He knows you.

29. How long will the non-believer be precious to God?

God says that His kingdom is a spiritual kingdom not bound by the constraints of the world. **30.** What is the advantage of that? (Romans 12:2) The spirit has authority over the physical realm. (Ephesians 4:20-24) **31.** How is your new self in likeness with God?

32. According to God's message to non-believers, what has authority over God? **33.** Which burdens does God want His son to carry on behalf of a non-believer? **34.** What does God long for them to do? **35.** What would you tell a person who wanted to give their life to Jesus?

(Isaiah 40:31) " . . . but they who wait for the LORD shall renew their strength; they shall mount up with wings like eagles; they shall run and not be weary; they shall walk and not faint."

(Revelation 3:20) This verse is talking about a personal relationship with the Lord.

God once told me: *I want to bless every single person. I feel such sorrow for those that have rejected me. Oh, if only they would give their lives to Jesus, they would have everything they ever yearned for, but never thought was possible. They would have the peace and joy that they have been missing. They would have an abundant and satisfying life and feel the love that they have been yearning for, my unconditional love which is free and everlasting.*

36. In the poem, IT ONLY TAKES THAT VERY FIRST STEP, why is your life redeemed and whole again?

THINGS TO THINK ABOUT BEFORE THE NEXT STUDY

Do I really trust God enough to protect me? Why or why not?

OT (Deuteronomy 31:8) It is the LORD who goes before you. He will be with you; he will not leave you or forsake you. Do not fear or be dismayed.

NT (2 Thessalonians 3:3) But the Lord is faithful. He will establish you and guard you against the evil one.

Meat and Potatoes

[People Hate Jesus]

I asked Father God how people can hate Jesus when they don't even know Him. He replied:

If they knew the truth about him, they would know that he treated people like they all wanted to be treated, with respect, compassion, and love.

Even today people do not know him, because my people have not shown them who Yeshua really is. How? By having the same character as him and doing what he did. Unfortunately, my own people do not even know who Yeshua is, because they do not have a personal relationship with us. You cannot really get to know someone without having a personal relationship with them.

My people are connected to me through Holy Spirit, but, until they wake up their spirits and seek to know us, Holy Spirit cannot show them the Truth, because their spirits are dormant. I can only have a personal relationship with someone through their spirit because I am spirit. The only way people could have a non-spiritual encounter directly with me is through a face-to-face physical encounter with Yeshua, he has the earth-suit. He could interact with people in the natural realm, but only one place at a time. To be with all our people at the same time, he must have a spiritual interaction with them. It is the only way he can be at all places, all the time, which he promised you. This is why he told his disciples that he had to leave so the Spirit could come to them.

The people of the world need a physical encounter with you, our mediators, to see us in action. They have no spiritual connection to us because their spirits are dead. (Remember that death is separation from me.) This is why Yeshua commissioned you, our people, to go into the world, you have the earth-suits to interact with the lost. They operate from their physical senses, so you need to approach them with your physical voice and body, showing them who Yeshua is as a human being, treating them with respect, compassion, and love. Only then can they be open to accept Yeshua as Savior and Lord.

When they accept Yeshua, they then can have a personal relationship with us, because Holy Spirit is in them and can show them the Truth, which sets them free from the constraints of the physical realm. Because they now have a spiritual connection to us and live from the spiritual realm, eternity, they do not have to be constrained by earthy boundaries, just like they do not bind me.

Please, Church, be part of my Ekklesia and show people our love so they will not hate Jesus, because they will see the Truth, and that will set them free. I want to spend eternity with them. I love them!

Study 27 – The Last Message in the Book

God has taught us many things in WAKE UP CHURCH! The main topic is how important it is to have a personal relationship with Him. He says it is the most important thing in our lives, for that is where eternal life begins. That relationship makes it possible for us to be who He created us to be and to do what He created us to do.

Pages (1st) 186–194   (2nd) 185-194

1. According to the message, why are there terrible things coming to the earth? God asks this question: **2.** Are you prepared to die?

3. Your spirit lives on, but where will it spend eternity?

4. God promises to take care of people, but what must they do first? We make the choice. God is not going to force Himself on anyone. Each of us decides if He is going to take care of us, or not.

5. What must people do to survive the chaos and unholiness that is in the world today? (2 Chronicles 7:14) **6.**If they do those things, then what will God do?

7. What makes it possible for God's people to be who they were created to be and do what they were created to do?

8. Why must you be willing to go where God needs you to go, to whom He needs you to show His love? Every promise made by God is for that one purpose: eternal life with God.

God says it is imperative that His people listen to what He is saying.

9. What is the DO NOT that He mentions? **10.** Why should you not do that? That is exactly what Satan wants you to do. Do not read the news, read the headlines so you know what to pray for, but listen to what God is going to do about it. Listen to the true prophets, they tell what God is going to do, not what humankind or Satan is going to do.

11. What does Amos 3:7 say?

The prophets are his physical voice on this earth. We are too, but often He speaks of what is to come through ordained prophets. (Ordained by God, not some religious institution.) He can give anyone of us a certain prophesy or message, though. We all must focus on Him and listen to His voice and say what He needs us to say, when He needs us to say it.

12. How can the time of turmoil and judgement be drastically reduced? That is important, because the longer it lasts the more damage is done and more people fall into eternity without God.

13. Are you willing to stand up to Satan's lies and tell him that he has no authority, but you do?

God asks another question that you should answer: **14.** Are you going to stop living from the worldly realm and start living in the spirit so that His will is done, and His love is passed on?

THE FUTURE OF THE WORLD IS AT STAKE.

God said that He wants to save a billion people in this worldwide revival. **15.** What were the next two things He said?

16. What is the last stanza of the poem I STAND WITH YOU?

Make this your war cry.

CONCLUSION

God told me that I should just keep learning and doing until it was time to release me. **17.** Why wouldn't He tell me what that meant? That is what He wants you to do.

18. In what ways has God pursued you? **19.** When you go out into the world as a royal child of God, humans may ridicule you, but what does Satan do? **20.** Why?

21. What was Jesus willing to give up so that we could have a relationship with Father God? **22.** What is the absolutely greatest example of unconditional love ever?

23. What does your soul contain? Remember you use your will to turn your switch up or down or off. **24.** Why is the Church so ineffective in ministering to the unsaved?

The most astonishing thing I learned was that God is NOT in control of the world. That is Satan's most effective lie ever — *We don't have to worry. We don't have to do anything because God is in control.*

25. Do you think the world would look like it does now if God was really in control of the world? **26.** If not, how would it be different?

27. What is the reason God is not in control of the world? **28.** Because you are a human whose spirit is connected to God's Spirit, what are you?

29. Why did God have me write WAKE UP CHURCH!?

We must stand together, united and committed to God's cause.

30. Will you join with us? Let us cut evil off at the root and change people's lives. LET'S SHOW THEM GOD'S LOVE!

The poem, GOD'S HEART IS BROKEN AGAIN, tells how both Jesus and Father God's hearts were broken when Jesus bore our sins on the cross. **31.** Why were they broken? **32.** What happens if we die and leave this world without answering God's call?

THINGS TO THINK ABOUT

What is the most impactful thing you have learned during this time of study?

Has this study helped you mature in your walk of faith? How?

Now, re-answer these questions: Am I a Christian? If so, how do I know?

OT (Psalm 119:1-8) [1] Blessed are those whose way is blameless, who walk in the law of the LORD! [2] Blessed are those who keep his testimonies, who seek him with their whole heart, [3] who also do no wrong, but walk in his ways! [4] You have commanded your precepts to be kept diligently. [5] Oh that my ways may be steadfast in keeping your statutes! [6] Then I shall not be put to shame, having my eyes fixed on all your commandments. [7] I will praise you with an upright heart when I learn your righteous rules. [8] I will keep your statutes: do not utterly forsake me!

NT (Romans 15:4-7) [4] For whatever was written in former days was written for our instruction, that through endurance and through the encouragement of the Scriptures we might have hope. [5] May the God of endurance and encouragement grant you to live in such harmony with one another, in accord with Christ Jesus, [6] that together you may with one voice glorify the God and Father of our Lord Jesus Christ. [7] Therefore welcome one another as Christ has welcomed you, for the glory of God.

Meat and Potatoes

(No middle ground)

So, it's a new year, the year of restoration?

(Smiling) That depends on whose side you are on. Oh.

Notice I did not say "or if you are in the middle." There are only two sides, no middle ground like most churches seem to think, at least that is how they act. You are either with me or you're not. Pick one. Commit to one or the other. How many times do I have to say it before my people get it? If you are trying to play the middle ground, you have not committed to me, which means you are not doing Father's will. You have not made me the lord of your life. I only did Father's will. After I was gone, the disciples did Father's will. Shadrac, Meshac and Abednigo did Father's will. Daniel did Father's will. They didn't say, "I only follow God on the Sabbath, so since today is not the Sabbath, I am not a follower, so you don't need to throw me into the lion's den, or the fiery furnace, or behead me, or beat me to a pulp and hang me on a cross. I, and they, committed to what needed done. Well, not Judas . . .

You loved even him.

Yes, as I do everyone who will not spend eternity with me. (Big sigh) Oh, my people, commit yourselves to me and do Father's will. Choose right or wrong, light or darkness, hot or cold. I, of course, hope you choose the Light, me. If you don't, well, I will still love you even though you will not be with me in heaven.

Is it, "I never knew you?"

Yes. The personal, spiritual relationship with me is only possible when you commit to me. When you commit to me you do Father's will, just as I did, because I committed to Him.

We commit to you by believing IN you; in how You thought, in what you said, in what you did, and in how You treated people while you were here on earth, and since we believe in You, we actually do the same things. Well, that's what we're supposed to do.

Yes, a doer of the Word.

A little Christ to the world?

Mmm, yes, but most religious or legalistic leaders do not like that term.

I suspect that they say it's, ah . . . Sacrilegious? Blasphemy, because I call myself a little Christ.

Yes, but they do not understand something. You have committed your life to me doing Father's will. You have a relationship with us, and we have become one in spirit and you characterize me now. If you do Father's will, people see me through you. Those leaders do not know who they are in me and will never know until they commit to me. That means they cannot do Father's will until they do that. Who gets to spend eternity with us?

Those that do Father's will.

To know His will, they must have a personal relationship with me, and Holy Spirit will teach them the Truth for he is the one that teaches the Truth. He teaches you through your spirit, so activate your spirit. That takes time, effort, and a strong commitment, but it will be well worth it. We love you. Pass our love onto others because we love them, too.

FINAL THOUGHTS AND MESSAGES

Thank you for implementing this WAKE UP, CHURCH! Study Guide. I am grateful and blessed that you have done so, however, more importantly, God is blessed by your commitment to His Word and to your relationship with Him. He has so longed for this. He loves you so very much.

Please do not stop searching for the Truth. God told me that it will take eternity to learn everything, and that, of course, means you will never stop learning if you stay focused on Holy Spirit.

Some people look at me as someone special, someone unusual. Let me assure you, I am not. I am like you, someone who knows there is something more and is seeking it out. We have all started from that place, that level of faith. I am not special; I have just learned more and grown more mature in my faith because of it. You will too if you keep seeking and developing that personal relationship with God.

It is not always easy. In fact, when you first start this journey, you will second guess everything. You will think to yourself that you are not worthy or capable to hear God, let alone do everything that Jesus did and more. (I'm still working on that part.) Do not let those thoughts deter you, it is Satan trying to lead you away from your spiritual destiny. He does not want you to fulfill God's purpose for you, because he will lose people when you speak out on God's behalf.

Keep pushing forward and do not look back, except to see how far you have come. I recommend that you keep a journal. It doesn't have to be elaborate, just write down your thoughts and questions that you may want to ask God. Write down anything that may come to mind, then ask Holy Spirit if it is from Him or someone else, He will let you know. I asked that of Him multiple times when I was writing WAKE UP CHURCH! and He actually had me delete two things because they were not His words but my words. He said, *"It is not because what you said was wrong, but because I do not want that said in the book."*

You may be skeptical about communing with Holy Spirit, just as I was, but ask anyway, just as I did. The more you focus on Holy Spirit, the easier it becomes to discern who is speaking and what is being said.

As you develop your relationship with God, the more you realize He is not the unrelenting, "old man" upstairs, but a personable, caring, compassionate, and forgiving God. He also has a delightful sense of humor. Here are some examples:

I felt as if Father, Jesus, and Holy Spirit was engulfing me. This was our conversation:

> I sense You all around me . . . like . . . (chuckling) a group hug. Now, that's cool!
>
> *(Jesus smiling) Hmm, it feels warm to me.*
>
> (Laughing) Oh, You . . . You are such a joy.
>
> *As you are to me.*

I had watched an episode of The Chosen. I commented:

> Thank You Lord for showing Yourself through video. That is truly awesome.
>
> *(Chuckling) The world ain't seen nuttin' yet.*

(Chuckling) A lot of "atheists" are going to be shocked.

Right out of their socks.

I use italics for God's words and regular print for my words. I started a conversation but used italics to write down something that I said:

I love You, Yeshua. Huh, I used italics instead of printing.

Uh huh. We both said it at the same time; but I said your name, not mine. That is why you wrote it in italics; you heard my voice at the same time you said the same thing.

I find that amazing every time that happens. Living with You is fascinating. It certainly is not boring.

(Chuckling) Well, I'm glad to hear that. I would not want it to get out that the King of kings, and the Lord of lords is boring.

I appreciate God's humor; it has lifted my spirit many times, but He still can get His serious message across, not out of anger or disgust, but out of love. It's amazing how much He loves us.

As your relationship grows, the deeper your faith goes. Holy Spirit will give you revelation on deeper things of God, and your discernment will increase, and you will be able to hear more spiritual activity. Let me give you two examples of that:

This first one happened in 2021 which was two years into my journey with God. I was talking to Jesus. I said this:

Many things are bouncing around in my mind right now. I think they all are from you, but I can't distinguish what You want me to write down. It's kind of weird . . .

You are picking up on conversations that Holy Spirit and I are having. (Smiling) It's lightning fast, isn't it?

Yes, I can't make out what you are saying to each other, but . . . wow!

Remember, we are all connected through the Holy Spirit, so sometimes you may hear my conversations with him.

Two years later I was more mature in my faith, and I was able to discern what Jesus and Holy Spirit were saying to each other.

I asked Jesus to help me with a project. This is what occurred:

Lord, can You help me get work done on the bedroom today?

(Jesus) Holy Spirit, that's your bailiwick. I give it over to you.

(Holy Spirit) Thank you Yeshua.

(Jesus) My pleasure.

(Holy Spirit) Though, you are the Master Craftsman.

(Jesus) Well, this is true.

(Me chuckling) Wow. It was astonishing when I first started having conversations with each of You, but now I am listening to You two having a conversation with each other, about me. That's totally . . . astonishing! How awesome is that?!

(Jesus laughing) Isn't she precious?

(Holy Spirit laughing) Yes, she is. Such a blessing and such a joy to teach.

(Jesus) Yes, she is a good student. I like her sense of humor.

(Holy Spirit) Me, too. She reminds me of you, Yeshua.

(Me) That's one of the nicest things anyone has ever said about me!

(Jesus smiling and nodding His head.) So precious.

(Holy Spirit) Uh huh.

My experience with the spiritual realm is mostly audible. I can't see into the spiritual realm yet, except in visions or dreams, but even those are fascinating. A few of my visions were mentioned in WAKE UP CHURCH! Each of us are different, and our experiences with the spiritual realm will be different, so do not get discouraged if you do not have the same experience as someone else. The Holy Spirit will give you what you need when He feels it is the right time to do so. He considers your level of maturity when teaching and giving gifts. Trust Him, He knows what He is doing.

The key to your growth is believing God's Word; you must study it until it becomes a part of your nature, and you follow it. This must be a daily activity, so that you do not drift away from God and stop doing His will. It doesn't have to be long and tedious. Pick a topic of interest and find verses that apply to it. If the verse references another verse, look it up. Ask Holy Spirit if He has anything to say about the topic. It isn't rocket science, it's simple. Here is what God told me about that: *My message is simple and worshipping me is simple. It is humans that have complicated everything.*

Everything in this study hinges on your spiritual relationship with the Lord. He said to seek Him first, then everything else will come. (Matthew 6:33) "But seek first the kingdom of God and his righteousness, and all these things will be added to you." You become a citizen of God's kingdom when you become a child of His. This means believing Him, doing His will, and living out the Truth just as Jesus did. Imagine how awesome it will be when He says, "Well done good and faithful servant, welcome home!

LOVE AND COMPASION FOR EVERMORE

Lord, I praise Your name in all the earth,
For You are the reason for my new birth.
Without Your sacrifice and all Your pain
There would have been nothing for me to gain.

I would have been stuck in this fallen world,
Helpless and fearful until I was hurled
Into a place without Your redeeming light
And no one to help me escape my plight.

But You, oh Lord, made the sacrificial choice
To give me hope and a chance to rejoice,
Knowing that You took my sin and paid my cost
So I could choose You and no longer be lost.

So I thank You Lord, with all my heart,
That You gave me a chance to be a part
Of Your beautiful kingdom, and opened the door
To Your love and compassion for evermore.

- Patricia S. Welsh

END NOTES

Cambridge English Dictionary: Definitions & Meanings. (2024), E. (2023, November 8). What is the Meaning of "Begotten" in the Bible? Christianity.com https://www.christianity.com/wiki/christian-terms/what-is-the-meaning-of-the-word-begotten.html

Dictionary.com/Meanings & Definitions of English Words. (2024a). In Dictionary.com https://www.dictionary.com/

Encyclopedia Britannica/Britannica, (n.d.). Encyclopedia Britannica, https://www.britannica.com/

ESV.org (n.d.). ESV Bible,

J Dermatol, I., Biswas, S., Surana, T., De, A., & Nag, F. (2013, November). Curious case of sweating blood. National Library of Medicine. Retrieved October 13, 2024, from https://www.ncbi.nlm.nih.gov/pmc/articles/PMC3827523/

King James Bible online, (n.d.). The Kings Bible-King James Bible,

LUST IS a CORRUPT AND IMMORAL DESIRE. (n.d.). Holiness Revival Movement Worldwide North America. https://www.horemowna.org/daily-devotional/lust-is-a-corrupt-and-immoral-desire

Merriam-Webster, (n.d.). Dictionary by Merriam-Webster. In Merriam-Webster,

New Testament Greek Lexicon-New American Standard, (n.d.). Bible Study Tools, Oxford Learner's Dictionaries/Find definitions, translations, and grammar explanations at Oxford Learner's Dictionaries, (n.d.), https://www.oxfordlearnersdictionaries.com/us/

Shrier, C., PH. D. (2002, March 1). The Science of the Crucifixion - Articles - Azusa Pacific University. Azusa Pacific University. Retrieved October 13, 2024, from https://www.apu.edu/articles/the-science-of-the-crucifixion/

Spillman, S. (2021, February 20). - ENTHRONED – YOSHEV- בשוי. Chaim Bentorah.

https://www.chaimbentorah.com/2021/02/hebrew-word-study-enthroned-yoshev-%D7%99%D7%95%D7%A9%D7%91/

Strong's Hebrew: 1984. לָלַה (halal) -- shine. (n.d.). https://biblehub.com/hebrew/1984.htm

Webster's Dictionary 1828-Online (n.d.) Webster's Dictionary 1828, https://webstersdictionary1828.com

What is a Covenant? Bible Definition and Meaning. (n.d.). Bible Study Tools. https://www.biblestudytools.com/dictionary/covenant/

**There may be references throughout this Study Guide shown as "OT" or "NT". These references are: Old Testament and New Testament. The verses are referenced using The Holy Bible ESV (English Standard Version). Any other versions of The Holy Bible referenced will be noted.